TO DO OR NOT TO DO: INACTION AS A FORM OF ACTION

A Convoco Edition

CORINNE MICHAELA FLICK (ED.)

Convoco! Editions

Convoco Foundation
Brienner Strasse 28
D–80333 Munich
www.convoco.co.uk

British Library Cataloguing-in-Publication data: a catalogue
record for this book is available from the British Library.

Edited by Dr. Corinne Michaela Flick
Translated from German by Philippa Hurd
Layout and typesetting by Pressbooks and Champagne Choquer

Printed and bound in Great Britain by Clays Ltd., St Ives plc

ISBN: 978-0-9931953-0-3

Previously published Convoco titles:

Dealing with Downturns: Strategies in Uncertain Times (2014)

Collective Law-Breaking – A Threat to Liberty (2013)

Who Owns the World's Knowledge? (2012)

**Can't Pay, Won't Pay? Sovereign Debt and the Challenge of
Growth in Europe (2011)**

"Enough is abundance to the wise."

—Euripides (480–406 BC)

CONTENTS

INTRODUCTION

Dear Friends of Convoco,

To Do or Not to Do, that is the Question. And the more I reflect on that seemingly obvious dilemma, the more I choose Not To Do. Not for contrary reasons, but in the end because inaction seems to me a good strategy in life and a beneficial focus for society.

Today, more so than ever, when being active means everything, the force of inaction is not to be underestimated. Only when one does not act can the power of inaction to bring about freedom be recognized. Inaction is actually conscious action, as the alternative possibility of taking action always exists. This is then not a case of unintended *laissez-faire* or non-doing, but of intentionally not acting—not-doing to try to reach a more distant goal, or to further a greater good. Inaction reduces and consolidates to the basic essential.

Haikus in Japanese literature, for example, express the essential in two to three sentences through a process of omission. In the same way, the greatest achievements are not a question of completeness but of stopping at the right moment. The key is not over-doing. Honoré de Balzac describes this phenomenon in his short story, *The Unknown Masterpiece*. For ten years the painter Frenhofer has been working on the portrait of a woman. He is seeking the absolute. Unable to stop, he paints beyond the point of completion and so presents a tangle of lines that ends up being meaningless and empty.

Inaction can break up and change power structures. A simple pronouncement—"I would prefer not to"—can be enough to destroy the consensus or momentum that produces power, because power generally develops from agreement.

Today, especially, such a conscious practice of inaction is an expression of freedom. Freedom always allows you the possibility to step back—to do so through conscious, intentional not-doing. In assessing things in our complex world, an ability to be objective is essential, and through inaction (in the form of abstraction and differentiation) we can best filter the complexity of our world.

We should note that stillness, a version of inaction, places great demand on actors. They have to jump over seeming obstacles to bring about that form of inaction. Psychologically, I would argue, not-doing is harder than doing. There is a biological bias that motivates the individual to engage actively when something can be achieved that is desirable, and that can create pause or non-doing to avoid something negative. To achieve something positive by refraining, the individual needs more discipline than through action. Thus inaction is the most challenging form of action.

Inaction implies not overstepping the basic freedoms to act. This creates more freedom for the individual. Seemingly contradictory—it is generally assumed "the more the better"—actually, "less is more" is also true.

In Christianity, eight of the Ten Commandments are pleas for inaction, as in "Thou shalt not…" This is the foundation stone of our cultural understanding. Often education builds on these principles and how they should be implemented. This limits one's own claim to achieving importance. It is how civilization develops and is sustained. A comparison between Ancient Rome and Ancient Greece shows the latter as the birthplace of philosophy, a land of culture, whereas the former is considered to be a civilization. In the forefront of a civilization are mercantile interests, goal-oriented action. Inaction is the basis of a civil society.

To act effectively, we show discipline by acting decisively, but in business we also need economics with restraint that rewards inaction. Ultimately we need action that does not have a negative impact. We are part of the whole. Man should not forget that he is a part of creation and not superior or unrelated to it. As John Donne reminded us, "No man is an island."

As change is always necessary—our age has shown that society is continually reaching new limits—we need to engage with change and actively drive it. A good strategy is to bring change by inaction, and to let Nothing become Something so it becomes productive as an action. "Not To Do" can, and should, be the way to go.

Corinne Michaela Flick, January 2015

This Introduction is based on the speech "On the Need for Inaction in our Society" which also appears in this publication.

THESES

CORINNE M. FLICK

Today, more than ever, practicing inaction can be an expression of freedom. It is always possible to step back—to distance oneself through conscious, intentional not-doing. One must simply make use of one's freedom and not do what one considers to be wrong.

WOLFGANG SCHÖN

Inaction can be seen as the expression of a concentration on the significant values of one's own life and as a sign of an attitude that testifies to the same respect towards others and their life decisions. But inaction can also be proof of an internal lack of mobility and weakness of will, and an external indifference or repressive tolerance. State inaction may be perceived as a crude offence against public duties of care, or as a noble resistance to the autonomy of economy and society. And state activity is judged by some to be the paternalistic enforcement of benefits, and promoted by others as an expression of self-evident social solidarity. Nevertheless the truth—to echo Bertolt Brecht—is always concrete.

ROGER SCRUTON

One very important way in which people can renounce the habit of doing things without also losing the virtue of responsibility is through membership of, and identity with, an institution founded on trust. Institutions have two virtues that individuals lack: they have long-term purposes connected, as a rule, with a conception of the common good, and they can learn from and embody the experiences of many people, including people who have passed away, leaving only their knowledge behind them.

BAZON BROCK

How can we turn not-happening as the goal of historical action into an historical event? What does the eventfulness of what has not happened look like by comparison with the eventfulness of what has happened? The problem of representing not-happening leads to the philosophical observation that "not" is not "nothing."

CHRISTOPH G. PAULUS

Doing and not-doing are sometimes very close. One can conceal the other. Particularly in politics this can lead to a seemingly active approach masking what is in fact inaction. However it is better to engage in not-doing in order to recognize and take the right course of action.

STEFAN KORIOTH

The approach wherein taking action with forward-looking legislation is the precondition of possible progress is no longer valid as it stands. The alternative of solving a problem by letting things happen, despite there being the option to take action, becomes attractive.

PETER M. HUBER

Ultimately, the Federal Constitutional Court in Germany could provide an effective contribution to the better acceptance of legislative and administrative inaction were it to delve deeper into the idea of the additional or cumulative encroachment on fundamental rights. This might also create a more manageable standard for the various burdens which are placed on the citizen by one or several legislators. The whole picture might then come into focus, with the possible result that inaction, when it comes to creating further burdens, is not only the most challenging form of action but the only acceptable form.

JÖRG ROCHOLL

If one tries to refine and concretize expectations of corporate social responsibility more and more, the belief might arise that everything is allowed that is not explicitly forbidden. This could result in an unnecessary amount of bureaucracy, publishing voluminous company reports on activities in the area of corporate social responsibility, and "ticking boxes," and thus elevating form over content. Such excesses would no longer have anything to do with improving the situation, but would merely lead to improved compliance on paper.

KAI A. KONRAD

From a global perspective a dynamic economy creates an important side effect. Only a technologically progressive, well-educated, and preferably affluent population can react with sufficient flexibility to catastrophes and changes in living conditions.

PIRMIN STEKELER-WEITHOFER

Of course inaction is not always better than action, and never in the literal or trivial sense of merely doing nothing. First, however, it is always part of the framework for evaluating every action. Thus it belongs, as philosophers like to say, to the a priori assumptions and transcendental conditions of every act. Second, in cases where certain typical reactions or actions are obvious, it is often very difficult to resist the temptation to intervene through actions or even just words, and leave things to take their course instead of subjugating these things to one's own will or keeping them under one's own power and control. This is often far better and more challenging than any well-intentioned action.

GERT-RUDOLF FLICK

In the fine arts the full application of all pictorial resources leads ultimately to a result that is not completely satisfying. Therefore some of these resources must be omitted so that the art work can maintain its mystique. In the field of fine art we can even talk about a commandment of not-doing, that is not applying all available resources. Great artists have always understood how to strike the right balance in this context.

FRIEDHELM MENNEKES

In silence, man plunges into his foundations and seeks a foothold in the "eternal now." Here—amid the fullness of time—the empty, sacred space imparts contemplation and stability, and shows the way where being unfolds itself into a question. It is the question as a question. Like silence, the question belongs fundamentally to the human self. Only when the individual looks into himself and redeems himself from himself, can he understand himself—in his location in space and time, in the question about himself and his freedom. Within spaces understood in such a way new attitudes and their inner commandments can emerge freely, even the enactment of a specific commandment of not-doing.

MARINA ABRAMOVIĆ

I see silence as an extremely important condition of everything because I think that it is some extension of any decision you have to take. So when you enter the silence of a space and you put this extra silence in your ears you automatically are in a different space, in a different zone. You are in a kind of parallel reality and that really helps people to focus.

CHAPTER 1

SPEECH ON THE NEED FOR INACTION IN OUR SOCIETY

CORINNE MICHAELA FLICK

Ladies and Gentlemen,

Today, I would like to reflect for a moment on the need for inaction in our world.

We all remember how remarkably this was achieved by Mahatma Gandhi. With good reason he said: "Non-cooperation with evil is as much a duty as is cooperation with good."

This slight, barefooted man, naked except for a home-spun cotton shawl, took on the might and pomp of the Empire in British India with a policy of doing nothing. In the face of violence and unrest he achieved spectacular success—he effectively toppled the Empire and brought about freedom, and the eventual creation of the greatest democracy in the world.

Inaction is only a form of conscious action if other possibilities of being active are available. Being purposefully non-active is not a question of unintended not-doing: I am talking about *deliberate* not-doing.

Let me explain this through our understanding of complexity on the one hand, and myths and superstitions on the other. Complexity allows the individual to secede, distance, or separate himself. Ideologies, myths, and superstitions, by contrast, do not allow this: we are trapped. Detaching oneself through abstraction and differentiation is not possible. When we are confronted by the full complexity of the world, the option of distancing oneself must be considered.

Remember the Yorkshire adage, "when in doubt, do nowt!" This is achieved most successfully through selective inaction—purposeful inaction as a general life strategy.

Today, more than ever, practicing inaction can be an expression of freedom. It is always possible to step back—to distance oneself through conscious, intentional not-doing. One must simply make use of one's freedom and not do what one considers to be not right. This is how one maintains one's own dignity—by not submitting to what one knows to be wrong. As the theorist Bazon Brock says, dignity is only properly due to those who know how to respect. One must even learn to respect nature, including flowers in the hedgerow or garden, for example, as well as what one crucially considers to be morally right, and this is how we gain dignity. This is necessary in all areas.

Take, for example, the realm of technological progress, which interests me greatly. According to Jaron Lanier—this year's winner of the German Book Trade's Peace Prize—we should be working towards a situation where "really efficient technological designs improve both service and dignity for people at the same time."

Equally, in today's world, our actions need to be effective. How do we achieve this? On the one hand, by not overstepping our freedom to act. This places great demands on the individual. Here it is useful to remember that reduction in choices and outcomes can also bring about consolidation and strength. On the other hand, we can aim to be effective by developing economies of restraint in which "doing by not-doing" is rewarded. The art of restraint has potential; it can deny power, for example. In such a way, the scrivener Bartleby, in Herman

Melville's eponymous novella, completely undermines the authority and self-assurance of his superior with a simple, repeated statement: "I would prefer not to."

And this is exactly what the concentration of power in the hands of individual businesses can achieve. With a simple "I would prefer not to" power structures can be fought and/or changed, as power accrues where there is agreement. Consensus fuels power.

Recently I read in the *Financial Times* how the Brazilian philosopher Roberto Unger described exactly what the think-tank Convoco has been about for me over the last ten years. He said: "The essential thing, the ultimate goal of politics and thought, is a bigger life for the individual. A bigger life—that remains the main objective...to increase our divine attributes, to have more life."[1] We must understand that through inaction we can gain more freedom.

Now I wonder why we all find inaction difficult? Why is it easier to take action rather than to wait and practice not-doing? Why do we lose sight of our long-term goals and forget one fundamental insight—"long fuse, big bang"? To Not Do is the ultimate agent for change.

Notes

1. Roberto Mangabeira Unger in *Financial Times*, October 4/5, 2014.

CHAPTER 2

ASPECTS OF INACTION

WOLFGANG SCHÖN

Who would not want to devote himself to the topic of inaction, and face one's own and others' not-doing? In July 2014 theologians and philosophers, aestheticians, lawyers, and economists, together with experts in media and management met for two days in Salzburg to discuss whether inaction can be seen as "the highest form of action." Of course, this did not mean discussing idly doing nothing, or a negligent failure to act. This was about deliberating the conscious waiver of something, perhaps also ethical renunciation, in short non-action that is deliberately controlled and for which one takes personal responsibility.

1. Can we even formulate a distinction between doing and not-doing? Are activity and passivity not equivalent to one another both practically and legally anyway? Is the doctor who abandons life-prolonging measures doing something active, or is he just not providing further support? How much energy does a smoker have to expend not to reach for a cigarette—is it greater than his immediate enjoyment? Perhaps Erich Kästner's words are relevant here: "Das Böse, dieser Satz steht fest, ist stets das Gute, das man lässt" [One thing is true: evil is always the good one omits to do].The study of criminal law above all has developed ontological, ethical, and pragmatic distinctions between doing and not-doing. And of course, as everywhere in the law, we can see gray areas between both possibilities of human action, for example in the realm of care for the dying. Nevertheless the blurred boundaries between doing and not-doing do not change the fact that both these forms of action exist in principle, and that active, willful intervention in the lives of others needs to be legitimized in a way that is different from a passive, laissez-faire attitude to others' fates and decisions.

2. From the outset, religious and ethical codes of conduct are designed to lay down a core of obligations concerning not-doing. Eight of the biblical Ten Commandments take the form of prohibitions. Alongside the devotion to one God, these prohibitions primarily concern respect for life and freedom, family and others' property. The primary role of these duties of inaction lies in creating space between individuals, and thereby obliging each individual to respect the other's person. German Basic Law [*Grundgesetz*] declares this personal dignity as "inviolable" with respect to public authorities, thus demonstrating a basic understanding of the relationship between public power and the individual citizen that is primarily focused on state inaction. Beyond this central sphere of legally underpinned duties of inaction is where the individual's freedom begins—and with it the realm of personal responsibility as well. The moral problem of "inaction," and thus also a possible moral evaluation of inaction as "the highest form" of action, can only be discussed in a situation where the individual has a choice and subjective decision-making power. Are there criteria in the freedom to act or not to act that are not legally binding, and perhaps even flexible in their content? Or is it often better to give the legislator benevolent access to these freedoms and remove

from the individual both the burden of decision-making and the right of determination? Might it even be necessary in individual cases that constitutional duties of protection oblige the state to restrict the personal freedom of its citizens?

3. At this point the central question for lawyers concerns state-led paternalism. Jurisprudence is not alone in understanding "paternalism" to be a concept of state and law that allegedly benefits the individual, sometimes against his will or even without his knowledge. This does not mean situations in which the behavior of some individuals threatens to harm third parties or public welfare. The prohibition against harming third parties is based on the aforementioned core of legal and moral obligations to inaction with respect to the protected status of other people and of the public. The "paternalistic" state is set up further to protect the individual from himself, to prescribe the "correct way of living" for him, and to counteract his short-sightedness. In this context economists refer pertinently to removing flaws in the "time consistency" of human preferences and human behavior—from today's perspective, advantages in the future (for example in the area of health) appear much smaller and less important than our immediate enjoyment (of alcohol or nicotine for example). Should the

state intervene in such cases? What sounds like inadmissible paternalism to one person, seems to another to be the necessary support provided by the welfare state. The second option raises the question of what a human being should be: is it right to see one's fellow men (and oneself) as strong, knowledge-driven, and strong-willed persons to whom one can confidently entrust the passage to their own future, and who can also accept and take on risks and defeats? Or does the individual not really need the guiding hand of state and society in order to plough a furrow worthy of a human being, and in order not to fail unnecessarily or even lapse into permanent failure? This attitude seems more attractive and derives perhaps from a more realistic idea of what a human being should be. But is there not the threat of a collective controlling of preferences that gradually undermines the individual's freedoms? How many restrictions cannot be justified by "good will"? And which government would not want to educate its people for a better life? It is striking that the study of constitutional law is dominated by skepticism towards the state's paternalistic activities. And yet, thus far, Germany's Federal Constitutional Court has never failed to accept a norm on constitutional grounds because it wanted compulsorily to benefit an individual.

In recent years in the theory and practice of legislation a "softer" form of paternalism seems to have come to the fore—a legal framework of "nudges" that showers the citizen of diminished capacity with more or less helpful information and attempts to show him the right way at important decisive moments in his life by offering default options. But when this soft paternalism fails, the hard, legal instruments are "unpacked" once more. A current example is the product bans in capital investment law, which are always introduced when all the legal duties to provide information to the private investor have not managed to protect him against massive financial self-harm.

4. How much inaction am I allowed with regard to third parties? Where does the duty to protect and not inhibit others' freedoms turn into an infringement of basic duties of solidarity? In principle the obligation to act is subject to rules and exceptions. It is both intervention in others' domains and the duty to use resources altruistically that require justification, not the simple omission of a helpful act. This has an impact in two ways: anyone who is obliged to act in the interest of a third party is thereby restricted in terms of his own freedom. And anyone who must actually intervene to the benefit of a third party in the latter's domain threatens to patronize the person

he is supposed to help. The necessary delimitation of this freedom is and remains above all a task of the law that gives legal priority to mutual inaction. In only a few, clearly defined situations do duties of altruistic intervention arise: these are the legal relationship of care between parents and children; the contractual assumption of risk by a doctor or a mountain rescuer; or prior human error (for example causing a traffic accident), all of which entail an obligation actively to protect the person in one's care.

By contrast, the law does not venture beyond the narrowly defined criminal offence of "omission to effect an easy rescue" to the extent of burdening the individual with general duties of solidarity. Of course the citizen must pay for the welfare state, but he does not have to imitate it. In a free society state-imposed employment obligations and traditional duties of community service [*Hand- und Spanndienste*] are abolished. Even the random "monopoly situation" of the hiker in the Alps who comes across a stranger in distress on the mountain does not impose on the hiker the guarantor's obligation of a mountain guide. It seems even more important for the safeguarding of the interests of those in need of protection that the individual be prepared to withdraw from his inaction on ethical grounds, and take responsibility for his fellow man who has got into difficulties. Even more important is the bigger question of how far duties of solidarity extend regarding the national community as a whole—do they extend to refugee ships in the Mediterranean or to victims of violence in Middle Eastern wars and crises?

5. Considerably more legal in character, and also more complex in terms of the many people involved, is action in the medical sphere as it affects the interrelationship between patient, relatives, doctor, and the community. Of course the patient's outcome and wishes are of prime concern. And yet there is often a lack of clarity in concrete results, for example in borderline situations at the end of life. Is the patient in control of the situation, or is mastery of his own fate too much for him both emotionally and intellectually? Are relatives always qualified to speak on the patient's behalf, or do their utterances belie selfish motives? Should the financial interests of an insurance-oriented community based on mutual support [*Solidargemeinschaft*] be put aside, or in the course of treatment does one end up in situations where further active treatment simply "is not worth it"? Here the law is confronted with extreme situations of an almost uncontrollable complexity. The law and the duty to engage in an open-ended debate, whereby the options

for action and the various interests become transparent, might provide some initial assistance. But even such an attempt at clarification will not always bring about a final decision. In this case, does the doctor alone bear residual responsibility—and does the doctor even possess the residual freedom to make a decision, whose outcome he does not have to justify completely to all other parties?

6. From the fate of the individual let us now turn to the wellbeing of nation states. Here the choice between doing and not-doing is often manifested as the choice between reform and the status quo. Frequently the citizen expects politicians to "take the plunge," and of course politicians like to announce that they will do so again and again. In the difficult day-to-day life of practical politics, in the wrestling between conflicting tendencies that leads to compromise, and in the debate with the forces of inertia resulting from decades of tradition it is generally only incremental change that is implemented—a politics of small steps.The citizen often experiences this approach as a kind of "patchwork." One always moves—so it seems to the spectator—from one disappointment to the next, and thus experiences politics as a series of missed opportunities. This leads to disenchantment with politics, often even to disenchant-

ment with the state. To some the modern political concept of "there is no alternative" has become the key phrase in a situation of intelligently camouflaged wait-and-see. But is a politics of small steps really such a bad thing if it is cleverly managed? Is the much-lauded big step not frequently unconsidered, ideologically skewed, or simply too risky? It should be the task of politics to give the citizen realistic information about where small measures are worth taking and where fundamental reforms are urgently needed. The conceptual starting point is always the status quo. He who considers the major reform more valuable than the smaller one will have to provide concrete evidence of this higher value, and will have to look at all the consequences. The reformer bears the burden of proof.

However, precisely this type of open and realistic debate between citizens and the political classes rarely takes place (and the media especially does not like to encourage it). Politics considers itself obliged to demonstrate an ability to act, and so grasps eagerly at measures involving merely "symbolic politics." The hyperactivity of those in public office can be seen in continuous announcements that are often reactions to short-term phenomena or debates. This creates continual expectations that are continually dashed.

In such a case, more "not-doing" would often be required; not the not-doing that affects action, but rather a not-doing that affects the making of demands and announcements.

7. So is inaction the highest form of action? Ultimately that old-fashioned legal saying "it all depends" provides the answer. Inaction can be seen as the expression of a concentration on the significant values of one's own life and as a sign of an attitude that testifies to the same respect towards others and their life decisions. But inaction can also be proof of an internal lack of mobility and weakness of will, and an external indifference or repressive tolerance. State inaction may be perceived as a crude offence against public duties of care, or as a noble resistance to the autonomy of economy and society. And state activity is judged by some to be the paternalistic enforcement of benefits, and promoted by others as an expression of self-evident social solidarity. Nevertheless the truth—to echo Bertolt Brecht—is always concrete.

CHAPTER 3

BEING AND LETTING BE

ROGER SCRUTON

Faced with an obstacle human beings strive to remove
it. Problem solving is part of our nature, an adaptation
that has bestowed enormous advantages on our
species, to the detriment of our competitors—which
means to the detriment of every other species apart
from domestic animals and parasites. Sometimes,
however, solving a problem is the worst thing we can
do. A mother sees her child playing in the dirt, putting
horrid things into her mouth, and smearing her angel
face with the detritus of other humans. She thinks of
the diseases to which her child is exposed, and of the
social disaster that attends the seriously dirty child.

And she solves the problem by forbidding her child to play outside or to stick her fingers in anything save the cleanest water. The long-term result is a sickly child, whose immune system has not undergone the necessary early apprenticeship in dirt, through which we humans arm ourselves against the ambient infections. What looked like a problem that could be easily solved was in fact one step towards the solution of another and far more difficult problem, for which it has taken generations of evolution to find a remedy.

A student of history, taxing his memory with the details of the Hundred Years War or the story of the Counter-Reformation, has a real problem with retaining all the many relevant facts. He solves the problem by visiting websites that contain the information, and in all his essays he checks the facts against the sources he has discovered. He has solved the problem of producing factually impeccable essays, and the long-term result is an incurably amateur historian who has no map in his mind of the events that concern him, and who must rush to his computer whenever a fact needs to be verified. The solution to his original problem turns out to be his real problem—namely that he has out-sourced his memory, and thereby lost it.

There are a hundred examples of this logic, which has sometimes been referred to as the "law of unintended consequences." By solving the problem of infection through the use of antibiotics we produce bacteria immune to antibiotics, and so threaten to reduce life expectancy to what it was in the 19th century. We solve the problem of tyranny by deposing the tyrant, and it turns out that it is only *his* tyranny that is brought to an end—the lesson for all of us from the Middle East. And when it comes to regulation, and the massive stranglehold of the regulative machine created by the European Union, then it does not need a philosopher to point out that the unintended consequences of regulating normal and free transactions in a market is to create distortions that may threaten everything. One recent instance is given by the regulations that prevented our water authorities in Britain from dredging the rivers, with the result that half the South West was flooded last winter, at enormous cost to farmers and to the wildlife that the regulations were supposed to protect.

Of course, it is not enough to respond by saying that, therefore, we should leave things be. Problems have to be solved for two reasons: first because we *do* understand the *immediate* problem and *don't*, as a rule, understand the long term. Second, because we are responsible for what is immediately before us, and if we are to be blamed or praised it is for what we do or don't do *here and now*. The mother who sees her child eating dirt and does nothing, with the result that the child acquires a fatal disease, will blame herself, and be blamed also by others. She won't be blamed, at least not in the same way, for producing a child with a weak immune system. The bureaucrat devising a regulation is presented with a clear problem that he must solve, and will be blamed if he does not solve it. The fact that his regulation produces other and perhaps larger problems is not his concern, for those larger problems lie outside his sphere of responsibility. (I give many examples of this in my book, *Green Philosophy*, since it is in fact the most important of our environmental problems: the problem being the disaggregation of problems, so that the solution to one is the cause of the next.)

To put the point in another way, we are answerable for what we do or don't do, and we are answerable because we are free. But this freedom binds us to the world of *doing*, and puts *being* at a discount. Sometimes it is right just to be and to let be. But our anxious involvement in the matter before us, and our awareness that others are watching, others are questioning, others holding us to account, ensures that being and letting be are second to doing, whenever a problem presents itself. "Don't just stand there, do something!" is the call on the lips of almost everyone in a crisis. It took an American President, exasperated by his busy civil servants, to reverse the command, and to cry, "Don't just do something, stand there!" But how can we know when it is right just to "stand there," and what kind of education is needed to achieve such a posture in times of constant change?

There is a well-known habit among Muslims of leaving the future "in Allah's hands." "If it is Allah's will..." is a refrain throughout the *Thousand and One Nights*, and even now, when death or disaster comes, you hear this remark on the lips of the victims. You might think that this is an exemplary case of "being and letting be," and so it seemed in the days of Harun al-Rashid. But look at the Muslim world today and you see that Allah's hands contain nothing at all. Everything is snatched from them, subjected to passionate appeals for vengeance, for punishment of religious and tribal enemies, for oppression of the weak and expropriation of the successful. Our foolish attempt to do something about it involved imposing on the Middle East the institutions that embody, for us, the long-term perspective—institutions such as democracy, nationality, and the secular rule of law, which have no stable equivalent in the history of Islam. Not surprisingly, the attempt has been a failure. For in a society that entrusts the long-term view to God all attempts to take charge of it look like a usurpation. How can God be content with a government that contains people who don't believe in him or who worship him in the wrong way? How can God accept a law that conflicts with the one that he sent to us through his Prophet? How can God expect us to assign our future to committees of humans, instead of entrusting it to himself? Add to those questions a general indolence when it comes to taking personal responsibility for anything beyond the immediate family circle, and the result is the Middle East as we see it today.

But let us turn to our own situation. We are not in the habit of leaving things in God's hands, and we pride ourselves that our lives are organized, both individually and socially, according to a principle of responsibility—*Verantwortung*—and that this idea is embedded deep in our social emotions. Philosophically speaking, freedom, which is the premise of all problem-solving, is itself a social product—it is something we do together, rather than something that we discover alone. We become free through the endless dialogue that binds us to others, which causes them to ask "why?" of our actions, and to answer that question when asked of themselves. We stand judged in each other's eyes, and strive to justify ourselves. We distinguish those things for which we are answerable from those things that came about by accident or to which we were coerced. We people our thoughts and our world with excuses, and act in everything so as to win the trust of those upon whom we depend, and to offer trust in turn.

All that is familiar, and it is, in many ways, the defining feature of the human condition. Taking responsibility for ourselves and our actions is not just a matter of cooperating, in the way that pack animals cooperate. It is a matter of living in another way and another light—the light of judgment. Freedom and accountability are a single phenomenon, seen from different sides. And this means that our way of being in the world is not like the being of an animal, nor is it just, as Sartre might say, a "being for others." Just to be at rest is to be answerable for that rest, to take that rest as something deserved. Painters are familiar with this fact. When you paint the portrait of someone at rest, his eyes focused on the spectator, his hands folded before him or lying on the arms of a chair, you are not painting someone who *happens to be stationary*. You are painting someone who is at ease with himself, not called upon to act or move, but also the kind of being who could act and move if required. That is why the hands are so important in portraiture: they are symbols of the resting will, the will that rests because it is able to rest, and because it is ready to account for its inactivity. Rest is something we achieve, by freeing ourselves from action. And it is only responsible beings that can be fully at rest. Indeed, there is nothing that is truly at rest in nature, save humans: and rest is something they achieve by arduous struggle, to be written on the hands and faces of those dignified citizens now fixed to the wall.

What I have just written, and what I wrote earlier about the Middle East, contain a suggestion as to how we can defeat the law of unintended consequences—that is, how we can acquire the art of letting be. We do this through institutions. We pool our several wills in a single will, the will of the institution, and devise the institution so that it can assume, embody, and act upon the long-term view. How is this possible, and what does it achieve?

Here we must distinguish a true institution from a bureaucracy—vital if we are to understand the legacy of our civilization. In a bureaucracy decisions are allocated to bureaucrats who are empowered to take them, but the bureaucrats are for the most part anonymous and responsibility is "lost within the system": if things go wrong, no particular person is to blame. In true institutions, when things go wrong, the institution is to blame. That is to say, it is responsible as a *corporate* person for the actions performed in its name. In my lifetime half of Europe was subject to control exerted by the Communist Party, which was the core of an elaborate bureaucracy, whose main purpose was to safeguard the Party's monopoly of power. It was seldom if ever possible to identify the individuals who took decisions in the Party's name, and the Party itself was never held to account for those decisions—it could not be held to account, in fact, since it had no corporate personality in law, and no moral personality in any case. It hid behind the mask of other, and fictitious institutions, such as schools and universities, which were themselves protected from the law by being granted only a truncated form of personality.

Corporate personality is one of the great achievements of the Roman jurisprudence, and has operated over the centuries to create a web of obligations and liabilities on which government and administration in our societies has been woven. In English law it is perhaps less well known than it should be that the concept of legal personality has been qualified by another concept—that of the trust, meaning an entity which holds property and makes decisions for defined purposes, but in which those who take the decisions have duties towards the beneficiaries without specific rights against them. When an educational or charitable institution is set up under English law it is usually set up as a trust, and enjoys a form of corporate personality through the law of trusts, whether or not this has been granted by some administrative decision of the state.

I mention those points because they are a clue to one very important way in which people can renounce the habit of doing things without also losing the virtue of responsibility, and that is through membership of, and identity with, an institution founded on trust. Institutions have two virtues that individuals lack: they have long-term purposes connected, as a rule, with a conception of the common good, and they can learn from and embody the experiences of many people. A British private school takes decisions, through its trustees, for the good of its members, past, present and future. It embodies the experience of generations of teachers and staff, and has a place in society associated with the character of the education that it produces. By being part of such an institution, whether as a pupil or a teacher or a trustee, you are identified with a corporate person whose reputation is bound up with yours. You can enhance that reputation or damage it. You can benefit from it, and feel grateful for the institution that provided it. It establishes a bond of membership that both constrains you and amplifies your power. To put the matter in terms familiar from the philosophies of Fichte and Hegel, the school is part of the *Entäusserung* of its members, of their becoming fully realized agents in the surrounding society.

It is precisely this, however, that puts constraints on the hyperactivity that is the vice of modern people. The member of the school, faced with a choice that, once taken, might affect the whole school, understands at once that the choice is not his. This, he says to himself, is the school's concern. And that means the concern of past, present, and future members of the institution, and of the corporate personality that they share. It might be a question of representing the school in a competition or a debate; a question of raising money in the school's name for a charitable purpose; a question of standing up for values and aims inherited from the school which are under attack in the media; a question of intervening as a teacher when a pupil goes astray, commits a crime or suffers a breakdown; a question of responding, as a trustee, to some advice concerning investment or an opportunity to acquire more suitable buildings. Membership, in short, *involves* you in decisions, but allows you to *hand them on*, without losing responsibility for them or for the processes of which they are a part. Hence institutions assert a delaying effect on human activity, as well as an educating effect on those who belong to them. They make it immediately apparent to the one who acts that there are *long-term* consequences, and *long-term* responsibilities at stake, and that he does not fulfill his duties simply by responding to the present emergency. It might be right to ignore the present problem, or simply to discuss it without a decision, as when you suppress your anger at a vindictive colleague for the sake of the school, or refrain from dismissing the Headmaster simply because he was drunk at the school prize giving and unable to deliver his speech. All institutional life involves a kind of amplification of the being of those involved in it, so that the sphere of responsibility and freedom spreads out beyond the realm of immediate action. And this amplification of being allows letting be to settle alongside it.

Indeed, it is what institutions are notorious for. After a time of success, they are prone to complacency, not merely letting problems be but forgetting to address them. Institutions can decline as much from inactivity as from hyperactivity. Their great virtue, which is the creation of collective responsibility, can turn in a very short while into their great vice, which is collective irresponsibility. Be that as it may, this does not alter what to me is their salient meaning for us in the modern world. They are the best that we have, by way of giving a chance to the long-term view. It is through institutions that people acquire loyalty, commitment, and accountability to absent generations, and a sense of the world as ordered by the concept of personality. Without them we have no way of deciding between the problems that we must solve here and now, and those that it would be a mistake to solve here and now, since we don't know the consequences of doing so. I look back on the school and college through which my own personality was formed, and I recognize, in retrospect, that they were the most important brake on my egoism that I encountered at the time. But I also recognize that I was a great problem to both of them, and that it was only the long-term commitment to their corporate identity that protected me from the no doubt urgent desire all round to expel this alien organism before it ruined everything.

What I have written above covers, in the simplest terms, matters that should be familiar to students of Hegel's *Philosophy of Right*, and of his beautiful argument about the place of the corporations in civil society. Many tough-minded empirical philosophers are skeptical towards the idea of corporate personality—it is a mere metaphor, a convenient summary of legal complexities, they say, which introduces no new kind of being into the world, and no new kind of letting be either. But maybe it would help to dispel that kind of skepticism by pointing to the existence of a very great drama, in which the central character is a corporate person: Wagner's *Die Meistersinger von Nürnberg*. One interesting aspect of Wagner's story is the way in which two impetuous decisions by two irresponsible people are both overcome by the logic of membership: the impetuous decision of Pogner to confer the hand of his daughter on whoever wins the competition for the Prize Song, and the impetuous decision of Walther to elope with that daughter before the competition can occur. Both are short-term solutions to deep personal problems, and both are fraught with potential disaster. But, thanks to the corporate emotion embodied in Hans Sachs the situation is resolved. How? It is resolved through the incorporation of the outsider, and the elevation of the individual desires of Pogner, Eva, and Walther so that they become desires of the corporate person, and can therefore be satisfied together. The whole meaning of the drama lies here: in this resolution, which translates individual ambition and competitiveness into a shared sense of membership, the long-term interest of society is secured against the short-term emergencies of its members. Distilled in the character of Hans Sachs is not merely the sense of responsibility towards the institutions that made him, but a profound awareness of the virtue that is "letting be." He too had a problem, and he let her be. It is on such people, as Wagner so beautifully illustrates, that the building of institutions depends.

CHAPTER 4

AGAINST EVENT CULTURE IN ACADEMIA: TOWARDS A HISTORIOGRAPHY OF INACTION

BAZON BROCK

Angela Merkel's 60th birthday celebrations have shown what we can truly call historically great about her endeavors. In response to a speech paying tribute to her, she commented soberly that the speaker had indeed given an excellent account of what had taken place over the previous decades. However, she said, much more significant were the historical achievements that she and other politicians had accomplished through not-doing, and through prevention.

What is unreservedly commendable about her political action is the very fact of saying this.

History is determined at least as powerfully by not-doing, that is by what did not happen, as by what did happen. But the positivistic source-fetishist, called historian, is only interested in what was actually created from the abundance of potential alternative actions, what has come to fruition as the "main event," and thus he remains blind to the fact that history essentially comes about through inaction as a form of action. Instead, historians make us believe that historical power is the exclusive province of those who do not practice inaction but who act, that is those who are driven by the categorical imperative to unswervingly make things happen. Little wonder then that politicians—with the exception of Mrs. Merkel—make this their watchword, always with a sly glance at their posthumous reputation, instead of keeping an enlightened, humanistic composure and trusting that it is precisely their not-doing that will be recognized as real historical achievement. The best-known example of this is the former German Chancellor and former historian Helmut Kohl, who in 1989 had unfortunately engaged in so little not-doing precisely because he thought he would only enter the history books because of what he did. He would have become a man of much greater importance if he had also followed the strategies of not-doing when faced with the blackmail techniques of the *Volkskammer* [East German parliament], instead of wanting to supply historians with fodder for their later reports that he had founded a state to rival Bismarck's unification of the German Empire. Let us remember that our Western civilization has progressed only as a result of agreement on what should be left undone and what should not happen. I call the West's strategic prohibition of destruction and self-destruction through implementing a, however conceived, claim to validity, "the prohibited worst case" [*Ernstfallverbot*].[1]

The principle of "destruction as redemption," on the other hand, defined by a kind of self-intoxication that legitimizes action, evidently follows the logic of martyrdom. It is inherent to that logic that it measures its own magnificence by the degree of resistance encountered when implementing its claim to exclusivity at the moment of action. Terrorism, both in the past and in the present, is essentially based on the barbaric self-justification of one's own actions when violating the civilizing prohibited worst case, meaning a rigid, uncouth failure to observe the duty of not-doing. And this is always dressed up in the rhetoric and assumptions of emotional culture-war strategies, according to which being prepared to destroy, and in particular to destroy oneself, serves as proof of the justness of one's own cultural, ethnic, political, religious, or ecological position. Legitimized by the idea of martyrdom, the violation of the civilizing prohibited worst case results again and again in the enforced realization of such strategies and positions, and thereby becomes a historical fact as the systematic destruction of what it allegedly set out to preserve and promote.

Indeed, all this is fundamental to terrorism in and about history. Real counter-terrorism can only function by creating a basic level of eventlessness, and is thus successful in the sense of being historically relevant if and only if nothing happens, if someone is prevented from converting his self-opinionated contempt of the prohibited worst case into historical eventfulness.

How can we turn not-happening as the goal of historical action into an historical event? What does the eventfulness of what has not happened look like by comparison with the eventfulness of what has happened? The problem of representing not-happening leads to the philosophical observation that "not" is not "nothing."

It is well known that cultural nations in the West, for example, draw on the aptitude of individuals to prove themselves to be members of social collectives by guaranteeing such collectives' claims to validity. This self-image is manifested in the fact that the members of such cultivated collectives have nothing to learn except how to control themselves. Characterized by Freud in terms of personal psychology as the capacity for sublimation, this functions in an even more important sense as the adherence to established rules. The most famous example is the Ten Commandments, eight of which solemnize the meaning of their observance as not-doing, such as "Thou shalt not steal," "Thou shalt not commit adultery," or "Thou shalt not covet..." etc. These are forms of action oriented towards inaction. For them to become effective, a collective acknowledgment of action through not-doing must occur in each case.

This necessitated centuries of practice in appropriate techniques of perception and representation. For example, we might think of the care taken by Shakespeare and subsequent dramatists in describing this form of action, care that by comparison scarcely exists in historiography. Louis-Sébastien Mercier's notion of Uchronia, formulated in the question "what would have happened, if...?" refers to inaction as action, but was actually only effective in strategic thinking in a military context. The history of painting also developed similar tributes to not-doing. Marcel

Duchamp provides the most famous example with his emotional farewell to painting as a gesture of self-realization. In this, his message was to develop thinking as a combination of representation and processing problems. Instead of ostensibly creating "works," artists should also try to see their works as tools in the process of cognition. Sitting and playing chess, according to Duchamp, outclassed any kind of expressive prancing about. Equally, the Biedermeier period, which was torn apart so badly by the past and present culture wars of artistic activists, demonstrates its successful adaptation to the prohibited worst case. In Biedermeier paintings we can see absolutely nothing of the generational programs and state strategies to please the people [*Volksbeglückungsstrategien*[2]] characteristic of the principle of "creative destruction" (Schumpeter), nothing of the "fury" and "artistic terrorism" (Richard Wagner) that the avant-garde in painting and architecture proclaimed with revolutionary gestures, even after 1945. By contrast Biedermeier style displays quiet modesty, stillness, and felicitous not-doing. Adalbert Stifter's novel *Indian Summer* provides a textbook example of this.

Thus there is indeed an art of inaction that one can get along with much better than was ever possible under the terrorism of "let's create great things, let

us make historical events!" The importance of implementing the arts of not-doing is shown in the criticism of a certain Karl-Heinz Bohrer when Germans
refused to go along with his warmongering during the
Falklands War. He vilified the "Mickey Mouse men-
tality of dwarf-like Germans." Bohrer's case is relevant once more, as many people are demanding that
Crimea should be rescued from the Russians in a similar way to how the English, Bohrer's heroes, recap-
tured the Falkland Islands after they were occupied by
Argentina.

In universities and cultural institutions, too, there
is an urgent need to refrain from legitimization in
the sense of the aforementioned martyr logic of historically significant actors. Since the 18th century it
has been accepted that the arts and academia should
not depend on cultural backing, and should dissociate
themselves from any cultural legitimization—also
from a duty of gratitude towards the nation states that
make their work possible by financing it in the first
place. That is because there exists no mathematics,
chemistry, or physics that is shaped by nations or cultures—whether Chinese, Jewish, or American—but
only universal, and thus transcultural disciplines. The
same applies to the arts and overseas trade as it does
to diplomacy. Academics, like artists, are shaped by

culture, language, ethnicity, and religion, as are all
people, but academic subjects and the arts are most
certainly not. It is precisely from this that they derive
their power that determines the whole of modernity,
that they can claim universal validity, which no individual culture, religion, or ethnicity can. The claim
to universal validity arose historically through the
attempt by empires or imperial systems to achieve a
halfway peaceful co-existence of cultures. In mathematics a language was developed in which laws of
universal validity could be formulated transculturally,
that is beyond any cultural or religious world view,
however brilliant it might be. With Darwin's discov-
ery of the functional logic of evolution it became clear
that the arbitrary potential of mutations and varia-
tions had to be contained. However, this also means
that even in social evolution we must take account
of the relationship between excessive possibilities and
their meaningful realization.

Necessarily, both cultural history and history in
general will have to be written from the viewpoint
of inaction and prevention. According to our theory
of the prohibited worst case, cultural activities are
always to be gauged according to the measure of not-
happening, the active not-doing, which is why in historiography and political forecasting even those

events that did not happen because they were pre-vented should be considered determining, great, or momentous. The history of what did not happen, the history of prevention, of inaction or not-doing must be developed from a political, social, and in particular from a cultural point of view.

Notes

1. See chapter titled "Der verbotene Ernstfall" in Bazon Brock, *Lustmarsch durchs Theoriegelände* (Cologne: Dumont, 2008), pp. 64ff.
2. A term used by Rudolf Steiner to describe the welfare state.

CHAPTER 5

HYPERACTIVE ACTION AS CONCEALED INACTION

CHRISTOPH G. PAULUS

A. AN INSTRUCTIVE EXAMPLE FROM HISTORY

In his most recent book, *Antifragile*, Nassim N. Taleb cites a prime example of positively understood inaction that he has taken from ancient Roman history, namely the military strategy of a Roman who lived during the Republic—Quintus Fabius Maximus. He is probably less well known, or at least less famous, under this name than by the epithet of "Cunctator," that is, "the delayer." He was given this name because the Roman Senate was completely at odds with his method of warfare. The Senate was impatient with the hesitancy of Fabius's passive military strategy, and so gave him this pejorative nickname. The behavior for which Fabius was reprimanded lay in the fact that during the Second Punic War he refused to attack Hannibal's forces, which were hugely powerful and seemed invincible in open battle, but instead ordered his army to retreat time and again. He repeated this tactic over and over, and as a result he ground down and defeated his enemy. Thus through this purposeful not-doing Fabius conquered his adversary Hannibal—an opponent who had previously massacred countless thousands of Roman soldiers, in particular at the Battle of Cannae.

We can draw several lessons from this historical example. First, one that seems—but only seems—quite banal: the clear definition of what is doing and what is not-doing is based on a certain degree of relativity. In most cases the classification derives from the observer's perspective: in the end Fabius proceeded in a totally active way. He withdrew his army time and again from open confrontation and brought them to safety. However, the Senate and general public perceived this action predominantly as inaction, that is of failing to attack the enemy directly.

Second, expected action or doing creates pressure to act in a way that conforms to expectations. Even today Fabius is known in history books by the somewhat unflattering nickname of "Cunctator," and this eloquently illustrates the pressure to conform. Fabius was the one who, as commander-in-chief, ultimately defeated Hannibal, and thus rid Rome of its most dangerous enemy. What may perhaps have been justified during the period of hesitancy was outstripped by the final victory in itself, and might have been highlighted by some considerably more positive-sounding nickname. Nevertheless Fabius was still known as "Cunctator."

Finally, in this positive outcome from the Roman point of view, we can see how important and essential it is for human action (whether in the form of doing or not-doing) and its evaluation that a causality for the successful event that has occurred be identified. For example, the sequence of events during this period of war on Italian soil makes it possible to establish a connection between Fabius's hesitation and his ultimate victory over Hannibal. However plausible the assumed relationship might appear, the concrete influence of Fabius's strategy on the final result cannot really be proved—whether there was no influence at all, only a slight influence, or whether perhaps it actually was the deciding factor.

B. CONCLUSIONS FROM THESE LESSONS

All three conclusions mentioned above are described as lessons because they open up important insights for the phenomenon of hyperactive legislation that I now want to discuss. A couple of brief examples demonstrate what I mean:

—That inaction and action are to a certain extent merely two sides of the same coin is a well-known problem, especially in civil law. If the preconditions for a legal liability vary according to whether one is dealing with an action or an inaction, a question arises (and is reflected again and again in textbooks) concerning the liability of an individual who, for example, has not erected enough protection around his yard full of pieces of sharp metal, with the result that children entering the yard injure themselves on the metal. Has he infringed the duty of ensuring public safety by not erecting a higher fence (inaction) or by having erected a fence that is too low (action)? Here we can see that the qualification depends on an evaluation. We might presume to say that this reflects a kind of legal quantum theory: it is a question of how you look at it, whether one sees and judges a real event as an action or an inaction. And of course both apply outside of the law as well: for example are the EU sanctions which were imposed on Russia in summer 2014 and subsequently an example of action or inaction?

—The extent to which the pressure of expectations determines human behavior is familiar to us all from personal experience. How many things does one do—or fail to do—merely because "everyone" does it? We are all familiar with the parental instruction to children, "*we* don't do that," and this is precisely such a preparation for conformity from childhood onwards. The following is well known too: the greater the pressure the harder it is to escape and counteract it. This applies equally to action that is called for and to inaction that is called for. Even on the grand stage of political action one repeatedly finds stirrings that create this kind of pressure to conform. Only a few years ago, for example, the call to go to war against the "evil empire" in the shape of Saddam Hussein's Iraq, a call that France and Germany resisted, led swiftly to their being labeled with the pejorative, contemptuous epithet of "old Europe."

—The following example is worth considering. There exists a tribe of Native Americans who live on a reservation in Northern California and who feel responsible for nothing less than peace on Earth. This is expressed, among other ways, by the men of the tribe who, instead of following the cliché-worn warpath, meet up in the tribesmen's house every evening and pray for peace on Earth. This is certainly an example of an action, but in light of the general ignorance (apart from just a few people in the world) of this event that happens every evening let us look at it as an inaction, to the extent that these Native Americans do not market their peace work publicly in any way, thus leaving the majority of the world unaware of it. We do not know whether these prayers have contributed to the fact that fewer wars have taken place in the last 70 years in Central Europe than ever before in European history, and if so to what extent. We are not able to identify the causality between these prayers and this extensive period of peace. This is considerably easier to do in the case of an action, for example the creation of the EEC and its development into the EU, although it is possible that both contributions have the same effect.

This last lesson in particular demonstrates why action is usually preferred over inaction. For anyone who wants to "score points," that is gain recognition, it is better to act. Notwithstanding the inherent risk of failure this is the guaranteed way of making clear and highlighting the causality between one's own actions and success.

C. THE LESSONS FOR BANKING REGULATIONS

Let us begin our story at the end. To combat the financial crisis, European and German legislators have together enacted an astonishing catalogue of over 64 laws and regulations in the last four years alone, many of which contain hundreds of paragraphs. The topics they cover are comprehensive: they extend from regulatory structures via risk management, derivatives, compensation, restructuring and insolvency, deposit protection, securities business, market structures, protection for investors, consumers and data, rating agencies, and the shadow banking system, to taxation. In this context, for example, the existing Financial Stability Fund was transformed into the Financial Stability Board, regulations were enacted by various regulatory authorities, the influence of ratings on the required equity ratio was limited, short-selling was subjected to a strict regime, a comprehensive law on the re-structuring and liquidation of banks was enacted, and a similar law on the separation of commercial and investment banking came into force, etc., etc.

The trigger for this legislative hyperactivity, and with it the start of the context of events we are discussing here, was the financial crisis, which after a few early warning signs, for example the collapse of Bear Stearns in spring 2008, first came to worldwide attention through the crash of Lehman Brothers bank on September 15, 2008, and the subsequent near collapse of the AIG insurance company. This brought the world to the brink of complete economic collapse once more, after the so-called Asian crisis of the late 1990s or even the "dotcom crisis" at the beginning of the 21st century. The Financial Stability Forum that had been founded in 1999 on the recommendation of the then president of the German Federal Bank, Hans Tietmeyer, in response to the Asian crisis had not been able to exercise the stabilizing function for which it had been created. Instead, within the space of barely ten years, two more, similar crises occurred.

So the Forum was changed, in name at least, while all the other countless laws were not universally remade, but rather many of them were kitted out in a different guise. Yet with the best will in the world and the greatest amount of application no one can learn the sheer mass of more than five dozen new laws. To put it bluntly, it is as if I, a layman, am sitting in the pilot's seat in the cockpit of a large airplane and have to make sense of the hundreds of instruments and gauges during the flight. The time alone needed to get up to speed on all these new regulations so that they are understood and can then be implemented in daily practice would mean such a huge amount of work that several sabbaticals would have to be introduced for banking lawyers dedicated to the study of these regulations alone. Legislators cannot be unaware of this, but they still act as they have always done.

Here we might ask ourselves what prompts legislators to lapse into such a mad rush. After all, this activity reminds us of an information overkill that amounts to a withholding of information. The suspicion is that we have before us an absolutely paradigmatic application of the lessons we drew from the example in antiquity. It is of course by no means a new or radical insight that legislators commonly use every opportunity to react to accidents or catastrophes of whatever kind by enacting a new law or refining existing laws. In the case before us the extent of the legislation correlates with the extent of the crisis. In the mad rush of legislative activity, however, the suspicion that this activity for the sake of it actually conceals negligent inaction becomes entrenched. This is the lack of action to design and present a fundamentally worked-out concept that is not just a reaction to current deficiencies, but that contains a solution that has been thought through calmly, not just for the current crisis but also for future crises.

If we recall the fate of Fabius, the conqueror of Hannibal, and in particular the insight that it is a question of perspective whether one regards his story as one of action or inaction, it becomes understandable why legislators have displayed this degree of activity. Indeed legislators assume—and they are probably completely right to do so—that the enacting of new laws is expected of them, and that these new laws are the visible and demonstrable results of their action. The relevant accompanying propaganda that this has closed the previously existing loopholes that led to the crisis does its best if not to create causality then certainly to suggest it. That seems to be enough, as the collective memory is clearly extremely short. One example will suffice: the failure of the Financial Stability Board described above did not lead to its abolition, but to the renewal of its mandate under a different name.

Amid all this action for the sake of action, however, the real roots of the crisis are not addressed. Of course it would have been better to proceed the other way around: by identifying these roots first of all through purposeful inaction—a merely putative not-doing—in order to be able to cure them in the second place through action.

These roots include blatant insolvency privileges which were granted to the financial industry as a result of intensive lobbying, and which acted as an accelerant during the Lehman crash. They still exist, indeed more extensively than ever before. Another root is the unholy alliance which the state entered into with the banks in its permanent and permanently growing appetite for money. By means of a carefully concealed (one could say without too much exaggeration, consciously hidden) legislative process numerous incentives are created encouraging the banks to buy government bonds—indeed to an extent that is way out of proportion with the attendant risk. This creates an interrelationship between banks and states that in the worst-case scenario means that the insolvency of one party leads to the collapse of the other. A classic example of this entanglement is the ultimate collapse of the Augsburg bank belonging to the Welser family, which was no longer able to cope with Spain's third insolvency during the reign of their "best" customer, King Philip II. Unfortunately several examples of this can be found in more recent history too: it should suffice to mention Ireland, Cyprus, or Greece (and to a certain extent Iceland as well).

The final root, left untouched now just as before, results from the failure ultimately—after literally centuries of inaction—to ensure the transparent, structured restructuring of sovereign bankruptcies. This root is intimately linked to the close relationship between public finances and bank financing discussed earlier. All the openly communicated attempts at a "bail-in," that is the strengthening of the creditors' risk-bearing, suppress the fact that the banks' biggest borrower on a regular basis is the state. Thus the misalliance is perfect: one side of this relationship sneezes and the other catches cold. It is hardly realistic to expect any relief in these circumstances, at least on the incentive of the parties involved. There is an enormous interest in leaving everything exactly as it has always been. "Leave it be" is another way of saying "don't do what is necessary." Nevertheless at the end of 2014—more precisely since September 9, 2014—some hope is burgeoning, at least in this direction. At the request of a large number of developing nations (G77 and China) the UN General Assembly passed a resolution which made it the UN's duty to make every endeavor to introduce an orderly procedure for sovereign bankruptcy. The catalyst for this resolution was a court case in New York which Argentina lost against a so-called vulture fund. In this action, in this legal victory, the causalities are clearly visible.

*

CHAPTER 6

THE LEGISLATOR'S INACTION—BETWEEN VIRTUE AND DEFAULT

STEFAN KORIOTH

I.

The subject "To Do or Not to Do: Inaction as a Form of Action" has many facets. It concerns not only human behavior. Institutions and societies, too, can behave actively or passively. The legislator that we happily personify has been accused many times of creating a flood of legal standards on the one hand, and of being responsible for problematic inaction on the other. This is not surprising, nor the result of a crisis. It serves only to strengthen the fact that legal standards are one of the central instruments used to manage modern societies. Whether they should be enacted at all or with what kind of content is always the subject of dispute. So are there criteria that determine when the legislator should exercise restraint or is required to provide clear demarcations and policy decisions in the interest of safeguarding freedom and the common good? In the context of legislation the theme of inaction and restraint acquires a broader dimension in light of the legislator's ever faster and more detailed reactions to new challenges. In addition, "the legislator" today comprises a multiplicity of legislative authorities, and this multiplicity increases the danger of standards being produced that are contradictory or poorly coordinated. In the case of Germany there exists, alongside the federal legislature and that of the *Länder*, the European Union, whose legal instruments nowadays clearly surpass national legislation in terms of both quantity and scope. In addition this qualitatively different dimension became evident as early as 1995 when the OECD, in its *Reference Checklist for Regulatory Decision-Making and Background Note*, recommended the authorization of legal instruments only if they are necessary and if the advantages outweigh the costs. In fact every act of legislation entails a cost—if only in terms of the effort and expense of the target groups who have to adapt to the new law.

So can we say anything general about when legislators should refrain from creating new legislation? Given the excessive number of laws in all developed states, should we value inaction fundamentally more on the part of legislators today than the active creation of legislation? That is, is inaction "more challenging" in the sense of our topic?

II.

It seems clear at first sight but the distinction between action and inaction, that is between doing and not-doing, is not so straightforward. Although the distinction plays a major role in many moral and legal debates—for example the highly controversial topic of active and passive euthanasia—in both epistemology and philosophy it attracted little interest until the 20th century. Only in the context of doctrines of causation—since Kant causality is one of the transcendental concepts of the understanding, as a category of relation—has this distinction invited intellectual experimentation: can not-doing be a cause of change in the external world? Or does this only apply to active doing that fulfills or works towards specific goals?

In any case, not-doing is not simply doing nothing. Not-doing means non-action even though possible or attractive options for action exist, or even duties requiring action that are legally or morally justified. Not-doing means allowing things to take their course, letting things happen, although the person who does not act has an idea or a suspicion of what can happen if he does nothing, and moreover that he could intervene and change the course of events. In various normative contexts and everyday situations we can judge not-doing positively or negatively: someone who does not return a friendly greeting offends or annoys the person making the greeting; he who fails to give another person in distress all possible or reasonable help incurs a penalty at least by "omission to effect an easy rescue" (§ 323c StGB [German Penal Code]). Sometimes not-doing is neutral: someone who does not react to a contractual offer does not want to do anything or enter into a commitment. Frequently a differential evaluation of doing and not-doing can be established: for example, while euthanasia through inaction is often legally and morally acceptable under certain circumstances, this is not the case for active euthanasia. The withholding of information can be assessed differently from consciously providing false information. In law the general principle is that no one *must* act—unless there is an explicit legal obligation to do so. In addition, inaction cannot in principle be attributed any meaning, and it may not be interpreted as conveying any kind of legally binding commitment. As early as Roman law we find: *Qui tacet, consentire videtur ubi loqui potuit et debuit* [He who is silent, when he ought to have spoken and was able to, is taken to agree]. It depends upon what happens next. To a certain extent it is logical that the good deed is often valued more highly than protection from ill. Section 13 of the Penal Code equates inaction with the positive causation of an illegal outcome only under certain circumstances: "Whosoever fails to avert a result which is an element of a criminal provision shall only be liable under this law if he is responsible under law to ensure that the result does not occur, and if the omission is equivalent to the realization of the statutory elements of the offence through a positive act." Moreover in this case the penalty can be mitigated.

Finally we should note that the relationship between a person's doing and not-doing can shift over the course of time due to technical or social changes. Technical advances such as automation and computerization force the individual into a state of passivity (or allow him to enter such a state, depending on circumstances), resulting in a reduction in the areas where action is necessary. Modern machines replace actions, and the individual is limited to supervising automated processes and thus to a form of inaction; he only actively intervenes if the automated action must be stopped or corrected. Modern cars can park themselves fully automatically and they can maintain the prescribed safe distance from the car in front. The driver is turned into a spectator. On the other hand, with growing freedom as well as growing self-determined realms of activity that are not shaped by convention, society, family, or institutions the opportunities for action rise, and in so doing the number of non-actions increase as well: "With every rise in the number of options more and more things remain undone with, among other things, the ethically important consequence that the pressure for justification that persists because of the non-use of the prevailing possibilities increases and the acceptance of what was formerly considered natural and a matter of fate requires moral justification no less than active intervention. Correspondingly, in order to lessen the moral pressure, one tends more and more to make a distinction between action and inaction: while it is still prohibited actively to cause damage, not everything one can do must be done to prevent such damage or to eliminate it."[1]

III.

Where does the legislator come in? Although he is exclusively a product of constitutional law in institutions, procedures, competences, and commitments, and then in turn produces the law, by personifying him we preserve something of the original mythological figure of the ancient law-maker, and we ascribe to him—as we would ascribe realms of creativity and activity to a person—reason and irrationality, high levels of activity and restraint, the potential for paternalism and tolerant equanimity. All these are characteristics that are frequently used to evaluate (non-enacted) laws. They incorporate the possibility of conscious and meaningful inaction.

The legislator promulgates or produces existing laws. In the historical development of Western culture his role has shifted ever more noticeably towards production. However, it is easier not to produce laws than to promulgate laws made by other people. Antiquity boasted great legislators such as Solon, Moses, and Draco, all the way to Mohammed, whose importance lay mainly in assuming the role of translator or

STEFAN KORIOTH

interpreter of divine injunctions for a legal community. The belief that laws are made (or can be made)
autonomously by people for themselves first gained
ground in Europe with the advent of Rationalism and
the Enlightenment in the 18th century. Until then
the origins of the law were considered to be divine
commandment, custom and usage, whether written
or unwritten. The law was fundamentally static, as
was society. The law was always old, and both good
and basically immutable because of its age. In the
Middle Ages consideration was given to the content
of the law, but not to its function as a legislative
authority, although secular and church institutions
and officials were perfectly entitled to create laws.

Only at the start of the modern era did we see the
emergence of the legislator who was able to make
laws in a dynamic way. The turning point can be seen
in the case of Jean-Jacques Rousseau. In his *Social Contract* of 1761 there is a remarkable chapter on the
legislator. This *législateur* is a person, although under
the social contract, which involves everyone, legislative power can only reside with the people. The legislator is tasked with coaxing the will of the people
into shape and into a system, submitting suggestions
for legislation, and ensuring the good sense of the
law. The "great soul" of the legislator should make

sure that the public spirit necessary to the continued existence of the community remains renewed, and that rational principles of community life are asserted according to the challenges of the time. For Rousseau the question of whether the legislator is a friendly but determined educator or merely the enforcer of the public remained undecided. The great codifications that began around 1750 tried quite pragmatically to shape as many life situations as possible, both proactively and rationally. The 1794 General State Laws for the Prussian States enacted laws covering all areas of life and society in over 20,000 regulations: civil law, state law, canon law, professional law, as well as criminal law. Having discovered its powers, the sovereign state wanted to regulate everything. The idea of inaction on the part of the legislator was on nobody's mind. The act of legislation was progress, inaction was stasis or even a retrograde step. In the 18th century the whole of Europe entered the age of creating "a legal basis for relations of political rule and social intercourse."[2]

The 19th and 20th centuries refined and extended the idea of progress through new laws. With the introduction of written constitutions in Germany in the first half of the 19th century, distinctions had to be made between the law and the constitution. The latter comprised the basic system that also regulated the creation of the rest of the law, whose production especially in the context of the monarchical state attracted particular attention from civil society. Through the cooperation of parliament legislative activity meant civil participation in the state, the regulation of interventions in freedom and property, and a realm of self-determination through co-determination. All this allowed no space for reflection on the desirability of legislative restraint or legislative inaction. Instead, at the end of the 19th century, the law was acknowledged to be the central and quantitatively growing instrument of control for both state and society.

Alongside the requirement to allow the state to intervene in the freedom and property of the citizen only on the basis of a law, there emerged another, initially undisputed area—the necessity for the law in tasks assigned to the state, namely financial or budgetary legislation. The monarchical authoritarian state that the law was to limit was then extended to become an intervention state, which regulated more and more areas of life and tackled social redistribution—through infrastructure, public service, and social security—as a task and consequence of industrialization. Since the Weimar Constitution of 1919, and unmistakably in the German Basic Law [*Grund-gesetz*] that expressly asserted the primacy of the constitution over the law for the first time (Art. 20 section 3; Art. 1 section 3 Basic Law), comprehensive, substantive commitments and instructions for the legislator as set out in the constitution moved center-stage. The act of legislation became largely the implementation of the constitution. At the same time increasing industrialization and its consequences and side effects, changes in the social strata of the population, urbanization, economic dynamics and crises demanded more and more standards in order to guarantee legal certainty and protection. The same applied to the demarcation and limitation of areas of freedom, social redistribution, the protection of the weak and of the environment. Ultimately it is the increasing differentiation in society, linked with the declining importance of social and cultural systems of standards, primarily of religious derivation, that demand legal regulation. New freedoms and threats to freedom created by mobility and an increasingly digital world require further legislation and regulation. Increasingly extensive EU laws are applied over and above national laws. This has brought about today's paradoxical situation. On the one hand the law is the central and indispensable instrument for managing and shaping the democratic constitutional state. Indeed the promulgation of a law can lead to profound reactions in its potential recipients or become a way of exerting pressure when governments or legislators want to induce a particular type of behavior in individuals and above all in social organizations and businesses. A striking example in recent years is the agreement between the pharmaceutical industry and the German government to pay holders of statutory health insurance hundreds of millions of Euros if the legislator dispenses with statutory price regulation for a fixed period of time. However, with the increasing number of regulations the law is clearly less and less able to exert control. The ubiquity of the law impairs its authority.

IV.

The consequences of the ubiquity, acceleration, complexity, and technical nature of modern law were described recently by the legal historian Michael Stolleis: "The legal system not only continually produces new problems and new standards. It must also liberate itself from standards through the systematic and ongoing discarding of norms. For the Federal Republic and the *Länder* not only can we count nearly 30,000 laws and regulations, but also an equal number of DIN standards. The rules and regulations for the electricity system alone comprise more than 100,000 DIN A4 pages. At a European level this all is turning into a paper nightmare that is then translated into 27 original languages by the largest translation agency in the world in Brussels. This accumulation of standards would grow even faster than it currently does if the permanent discarding of norms did not indeed exist."[3]

It is obvious that in this situation the legislator's inaction becomes an interesting form of behavior. The previous approach, wherein taking action with forward-looking legislation is the precondition of possible progress, is no longer valid as it stands. The alternative of solving a problem by letting things happen, despite there being the option to take action, becomes attractive. A good example is the privatization of activities that were hitherto the province of the state—telecommunications, rail transport, garbage collection, and energy provision. The retreat of the state and the liberation and use of social forces were the obvious response to an excessive and overburdened state that was supposed to develop from an active to an activating state. In some areas this worked well, in others less so. In all cases, however, the hope of being able to regress the concentration of legal standardization was difficult to implement because of expected or unexpected side effects.

The freedoms created by the law have to be accompanied by complicated frameworks and regulations. In highly diversified societies the legislator must be able to judge precisely when the production of laws can be set to standby mode. Inactive legislation shifts or preserves the distribution of power within society—and for the distribution of competences within the state it means the creation of extended spheres of action for the judiciary and administration. Ultimately the law is the instrument for substantively guiding and democratically legitimizing the second and third estates. However, the retreat of the law and the equanimity of the legislator also require a justifiable faith in the ability of society to govern itself—the financial and banking crisis that began in 2008 has deprived us of a degree of hope in this regard. In spite of these fundamental doubts, inaction has some productive potential against a backdrop of highly differentiated systems. Law is always the attempt to give the past and present dominance over the future—however the less the future is obstructed the better. In the case of uncertainty, too, letting things happen and waiting can—and not must—be the legislator's considered response. Acting too early can perpetuate uncertainty. It is not just excessive laws that weaken the authority of necessary laws and of the legislator; unsure and half-hearted problem-solving in setting standards also creates this effect.

However, there are also situations when the legislator must act. A first group is unproblematic: on many occasions the Basic Law tasks the legislator with providing regulations concerning details, for example in laws concerning political parties and elections (Arts. 21, 38 Basic Law). Other laws give the legislator a general task, for example concerning the protection of the family and children (Art. 6 Basic Law) or of the environment (Art. 20a Basic Law). Here the constitution indicates that it wants to be a framework that offers the legislator scope that he must then, however, use. In the case of elections to the Bundestag, the constitution leaves it up to the legislator whether a system of proportional representation or of first-past-the-post is required. It is also left to the legislator's political discretion whether he wants to protect the environment by prohibiting behavior, or by softer systems of encouragement such as environmental levies. A second group of possible regulatory tasks is more problematic. The Federal Constitutional Court's caselaw derives from the constitutional duty of protection—that in certain circumstances the law is necessary to make protection effective. The basic right to life and physical integrity (Art. 2 section 2 clause 1 Basic Law) demands that the state strive to preserve life as a protector and supporter, which means above all to preserve life from the illegal interventions of others. For example—although the case-law of the Federal Constitutional Court has become variable here—the application of penal law might be desirable for the effective implementation of the fundamental prohibition of abortion (§ 218 Penal Code). Also, for example, when dealing with the dangers associated with the peaceful use of nuclear energy, the legislator would have to guarantee an effective legal level of protection. Here, once again, we see quite clearly the problem of the duty of action that wants to exclude inaction: beyond obvious examples—protecting the citizen from danger is a basic task of the state—regulatory obligations are gateways to the limitation of freedom. The protection of one individual is linked to the limitation of the freedom of the other; asserting a duty of protection diverts attention from the intervention into the rights of others. Duties of action are gateways to a paternalistic legislator. By contrast we should remember that in a free society, any law that obstructs options for action requires justification. More generally, anyone who wants to change the status quo, bears the burden of proof. New legislation is meaningful if it either improves the situation of everyone, or if this is not the case, good reasons can be given why such legislation should nevertheless be passed. In Montesquieu's *The Spirit of Laws* (1748) it is expressed thus: without sufficient grounds no changes may be made to the law. Montesquieu's work is also a treasure trove on this topic in other respects. Chapter 6 in Book XIX bears the wonderful title "That Everything Ought Not to be Corrected" (the emphasis on the "ought"). "Let them but leave us as we are, said a gentleman […], and nature will repair whatever is amiss. She has given us a vivacity capable of offending, and hurrying us beyond the bounds of respect: this same vivacity is corrected by the politeness it procures us, inspiring a taste for the world […]. Let them leave us as we are: our indiscretions joined to our good nature, would make the laws which should constrain our sociable temper, not at all proper for us." This timeless insight can be combined with one that is of its time. Through inaction, the legislator helps dismantle the excesses inherent in the omnipresent process of regulation.

Notes

1. Dieter Birnbacher, *Tun und Unterlassen* (Stuttgart: Reclam, 1995), p. 47.

2. Jürgen Osterhammel, *The Transformation of the World: A Global History of the Nineteenth Century*, trans. Patrick Camiller (Princeton NJ: Princeton University Press, 2014), p. 904.

3. Michael Stolleis, "Vom Umgang mit veralteten Büchern, oder: mit den Toten sprechen" in Jakob Nolte et al., (eds.), *Die Verfassung als Aufgabe von Wissenschaft, Praxis und Öffentlichkeit. Freundesgabe für Bernhard Schlink zum 70. Geburtstag* (Heidelberg: C.F. Müller, 2014), pp. 15f.

CHAPTER 7

LEGAL AND POLITICAL
REFLECTIONS ON INACTION

PETER M. HUBER

I. INACTION'S LACK OF ATTRACTIVENESS

At first sight the notion that inaction, i.e. to do nothing, is the most challenging form of action seems
somewhat unsettling. Surely the old ironic saying is
that only he who does nothing makes no mistakes,
thus maintaining a clear opposition to laziness and
indecision. As far as politics and law are concerned
the following seems obvious: do we not expect our
politicians, as elected representatives, to stand up for
projects and reforms and try to put them into effect?

Don't we want them to change the status quo in order to make both state and society more comfortable and sustainable? Do we not measure their success above all by how many draft laws they have introduced and implemented? Is it not the case that a government's results typically reside in the schedule of laws enacted during its term of office? Is it not an expression of a lack of leadership, a lack of ideas, or indifference if politicians choose to "sit out" problems—from personal scandals via shortcomings in domestic or foreign security to the challenges posed by Google or the NSA? In recent times we have even been experiencing an increased tendency towards "symbolic legislation," i.e. enacting laws even though no one expects them to alter reality in any tangible way.[1] The more helpless politics is in the face of a particular challenge, the more it seems to tend towards action for the sake of it. In any event, for politics and the democratic legislators who dominate it, inaction does not seem to be a serious option.

The same applies, *mutatis mutandis*, to government and administration as well. If the official monitoring of banks, pharmaceuticals manufacturers or the food industry is patchy, if the police presence in public spaces, at borders, or in the context of traffic control is too scant, or if children and young people are put

in danger because youth welfare offices are not looking after them thoroughly enough, the executive must
expect that it will be accused of providing insufficient
personnel and equipment, of incompetence, or even
of corruption. Citizens expect action from the state
in general and from the executive in particular, not
apathetic inaction. Politics wants to demonstrate—whether actual or alleged—"successes," for
example higher academic quotas in education policy,
and plunges into action for the sake of it even if education, science, and the future prospects of students
were better served by not-doing, that is by continuity
and reliable planning.[2]

Even in the area of justice, activism—that is
decision-making—is regarded more favorably than
inaction. A district court judge who delivers lots of
settlements can be sure of the acknowledging nod
and a wink from his superiors and colleagues and
can expect a slap on the back. Of course, in the plain
light of day, praise for a high number of settlements
brings with it the suggestion that one is not proficient
enough for the "proper" handling of cases according
to all the rules of the lawyer's art. A settlement may
serve peace under the law. However the law can only
be successfully developed if suitable cases also come

before the supreme and constitutional courts, or the European Court of Justice.

So if we look at the reality of politics and law, the notion of inaction as the most challenging form of action seems to have something counterfactual about it. In any case it has nothing to do with the idealization of idleness.

II. CONDITIONS FOR THE SUCCESS OF POLITICAL POWER

If we are looking for the causes of politics' tendency to make its mark through active doing and to take refuge, when in doubt, in action for the sake of it rather than remaining inactive, this has something to do with the conditions of success and communication in political power within representative democracy, and with the struggle to win or lose power.

As general political, social, ecological, and cultural conditions change continually, the public welfare has to be constantly reassessed, interests have to be balanced and decisions about political preferences must permanently be adjusted. Under these conditions, promoting the maintenance of the status quo, i.e. inaction, is not a long-term alternative, as the changing general conditions affect members of a society in quite different ways. The political self-determination of the individual and of society, as laid down in the inviolability of human dignity (in Art. 1 para. 1 of the *Grundgesetz* [GG – Basic Law of Germany]) and in the democratic principles (in Art. 20 paras. 1 and 2 GG), also insists on adjustments and changes in politics and the law in this respect. To the extent that democracy thrives on the shift between majority and minority, as a rule those in political responsibility must demonstrate through active engagement and identifiably causal contributions that it is their job to master challenges and improve the status quo. The promotion of inaction—maintaining the status quo—is considered more a hangover from the *ancien régime* than the conditions by which a living, representative democracy operates.

III. ACTION FOR THE SAKE OF ACTION AND GENERAL INSTITUTIONAL CONDITIONS

The way institutions work also favors action, if not even legislative action for the sake of action. In particular, federal systems based on a decentralized execution of central laws, as in Germany or the European Union (Arts. 83ff. and 104a para. 1 GG; Art. 5 paras. 1 and 2 TEU; Art. 2 para. 6 TFEU), have proved to be particularly problematic in this respect. This is because they allow the legislature at federal as well as EU level to draw up regulations without having to provide for their implementation or financing. He who can buy without paying will find it easy to buy.

In Berlin and Brussels this has created a tendency towards action for the sake of it, an inclination that easily sets its sights on legal regulation without bothering about the consequences for implementation or financing. Nor does it take account of the overall burden on citizens and businesses: indeed, given the plurality of the authorities who are entitled to set standards (municipality, administrative district, *Land*, nation state, and EU) and the lack of coordination between them, this seems not only likely, it is inevitable.

This trend has been ongoing for decades now, and at first sight its consequences are barely detectable, but on closer inspection they are dramatic: over-regulation and bureaucratization, loss of coherence in the legal system, uncertainty and high transaction costs in the legal sphere, "petrification" of the body of law and a loss of flexibility, a drop in the opportunities for action at individual political levels, erosion of responsibility at such levels, and in the medium to long term a loss of trust in and acceptance of democracy and the constitutional state.

IV. THEORETICAL VIEWS AND PRACTICAL APPROACHES

Against this background it is remarkable that a theoretical view of the value of inaction and its particular demands exists at all. Montesquieu's famous dictum, "If it is not absolutely necessary to create a new law, it is absolutely necessary not to create a new law,"[3] belongs to the standard repertoire of every speech on state theory. Echoing these sentiments precisely, the German Chancellor, responding to the speech given in her honor on the occasion of her 60th birthday, invited her audience to consider how much damage had been avoided by the very fact that people had not made decisions.

This view has pervaded public policy as well. It is demonstrated by the existence of the regulatory control council set up by the Federal Chancellery, whose job is to support the federal government when implementing measures to reduce bureaucracy and improve law-making (§ 1 section 2 Act on the Establishment of the National Regulatory Control Council [NKRG]). The council is also tasked with checking new regulations concerning citizens, the economy and public administration for their comprehensibility and procedural correctness, as well as showing the business costs for medium-sized companies in particular (§ 1 section 2 NKRG). The idea behind this council is to avoid the creation of superfluous standards that are always associated with incursions into the freedom and assets of citizens and businesses. The law came into force on August 18, 2006. Whether it has fulfilled its expectations remains to be seen.

A similar tack was taken by former Bavarian minister-president Stoiber in his high-level group on reducing bureaucracy in the European Commission (2009–14), which submitted to the Commission on its own terms several hundred recommendations for reducing bureaucracy which would alleviate the burden on European businesses by a total of around 41 billion euros.[4]

As one of its first acts, the new EU Commission under President Jean-Claude Juncker cancelled a series of initiatives taken by the Commission under Barroso; and the Free State of Bavaria prides itself on having reduced the number of state regulations from 1,630 to 1,048 between the years 2000 and 2013, as well as operating a regular five-year overhaul of laws, sunset clauses, and a so-called *"Paragraphenbremse,"* a brake applied to legislative activity.[5]

V. POSSIBLE APPROACHES

1. Indispensable Obligations to Act

Of course there are also plenty of objective obligations to act that do not countenance the inaction of state actors. If internal or external security or environmental sustainability are in immediate danger fundamental state aims are at stake and with them the existence of state and society. In this case inaction cannot be the most challenging form of action but is more akin to cynical inaction in the style of Emperor Nero. Obligations to act can also result from the legislature's duty to protect,[6] the imperative of the welfare state, the transfer of sovereignty rights, or from general institutional conditions concerning the separation of powers in the constitutional state, the federal state, or the European multi-level system. In this case the action of those in positions of responsibility triggers obligations to act in others that cannot be dealt with adequately through a simple attitude of refusal. If legislators, the administration, or subordinate authorities no longer adhere to judicial decisions, this calls the system into question. When German *Länder* no longer loyally enact federal laws according to Art. 83ff GG, as for example with regard to nuclear energy in the case of the so-called *ausstiegsorientierten Gesetzesvollzug* [implementation of the law oriented towards phasing out nuclear energy] during the 1980s,[7] and in the *ausstiegstorpedierenden Gesetzesvollzug* [implementation of the law oriented towards frustrating the phasing out] of the 2000s,[8] this threatens the existence of the federal state. Equally, when the Member States of the European Union absolutely refuse to implement guidelines according to Art. 288 section 3 Treaty on the Functioning of the European Union, this threatens the existence of the European Union as a community based on the rule of law. Even if a single measure might be considered a miscarriage of justice, a wrong policy, or unnecessary bureaucratic micromanagement, as seen in enormous quantities in the secondary legislation of the EU (light bulbs or the Package Travel Directive, to name but two of many), inaction in this case is not the most challenging form of action but a challenge to the system.

2. Instruments for Making Theoretical Views Operational

In light of all this, the main reasons for the ineffectiveness of theoretical views on inaction in politics and law are the conditions of success that affect political power in representative democracies, the general institutional conditions of the constitutional state, and the increasing loss of a political center of gravity that can direct regulation at all levels and take responsibility for this with respect to the electorate. To change the structures in such a way that the incentives to legislative and administrative action for the sake of action are reduced, one should start with four remedies:

a) The structural tendency of representative democracy towards action for its own sake can be halted at least to a certain extent by referenda. Such referenda, as enacted according to the Bavarian Constitution (Art. 75 section 2 clause 2 Bavarian Constitution) or the Constitution of Hesse (Art. 123 section 2 Constitution of Hesse) in the case of constitutional changes, prevent the bypassing of the "constructive vote of no confidence" (Hegel) that is required to justify change. They leave the "burden of argument" (Martin Kriele) upon those who want a change, as they force a debate on the pros and cons of the change, unless—as has become common in Bavaria—several constitutional changes are put to the vote all together and the ratio of direct democracy is thus taken to absurd levels. In the case of certain financial laws, this can also be a suitable instrument if voters (can) recognize the interdependence between new expenditure and their own financial burden, as experiences in Switzerland demonstrate.

b) In schools and universities, in public administration and regions, in the police and the army, a continual actionist challenge to the status quo has become customary and works increasingly to the detriment of these institutions' effectiveness. Of course all these spheres need continual evaluation and reform—*eccle-*

sia semper reformanda applies to any institution. However, they also and primarily need a certain degree of continuity that excludes continual upheavals. To this extent the collective agreement regarding "peace of the school" in North Rhine-Westphalia is a positive step towards a challenging form of inaction; another instrument might be the establishment of certain basic decisions within the constitution.[9]

c) To a certain extent in the context of Europeanization and globalization the erosion of the nation state as a political center of gravity is unavoidable. However, the biggest deficiencies were compensated for by a more concise representation of the Member States at the European Council and at the Council of the European Union. This can (help to) avoid unnecessary standardization. In addition, the principle of conferral of competences, whereby the European Union shall only act within the limits of the competences conferred upon it (Art. 5 sections 1 and 2 TEU; Art. 2 section 6 TFEU), and the principle of subsidiarity (Art. 5 section 1 clause 2 TEU) would lend added emphasis. Although this is clearly very hard for Germany as a federal state, and a party state as well, it will be more and more necessary to make the political and intellectual effort to formulate specific policy aims coherently and evaluate the results, rather than con-

tinuing with the disastrous tendency to pass European legislation such as the Council Framework Decision on the European Arrest Warrant first, and then
expect the machinery of the constitutional state to
sort it out.[10] One might also attempt to maintain the
unity of the legal system as far as possible; it would
avoid unnecessary burdens on citizens and businesses
if EU regulations and edicts came upon the country
less like an unpredictable weather system. They
would be subject to a greater political requirement of
justification and be seen for what they are: a consequence of the actions of national politicians as well.
Instruments designed to do this exist in Germany
(Art. 23 sections 2 to 6 GG; Federal Act on Cooperation between the Federal Government and the German Bundestag in Matters concerning the European
Union [EUZBBG]; Federal Act on Cooperation
between the Federal Government and *Länder* in Matters concerning the European Union [EUZBLG]; Federal Act on the Exercise by the Bundestag and by the
Bundesrat of their Responsibility for Integration in
Matters concerning the European Union [Responsi-
bility for Integration Act] [IntVG]) and in other Member States. Of course they are hardly ever used, as then
domestic politics would also have to take responsibility for European decisions or at least some element

of them, which from the perspective of winning and losing power comes with additional risks and is thus not particularly attractive. Whether this is accepted depends both on public opinion and on the self-sufficiency of the electorate.

d) Ultimately the constitutional lawyer as well as the Federal Constitutional Court could provide an effective contribution to a better acceptance of legislative and administrative inaction were they to delve deeper into the idea of the additional or cumulative encroachment on fundamental rights.[11] This might also create a more manageable standard for the various burdens which are placed on the citizen by one or several legislators. The whole picture might then come into focus, with the possible result that inaction, when it comes to creating further burdens, is not only the most challenging form of action but the only acceptable form.

Notes

1. In the area of constitutional law as applied to German *Länder,* see Peter M. Huber, "Bundesverfassungsrecht und Landesverfassungsrecht" in *Niedersächsischen Verwaltungsblätter* [*NdsVBl.*] (2011), p. 233 (238).

2. Peter M. Huber, *Staat und Wissenschaft* (Paderborn: Schön-ingh, 2008), pp. 13 f.

3. Montesquieu, *The Spirit of Laws. A Compendium of the First English Edition*. Edited with an introduction, notes, and appendixes by David Wallace Carrithers (Berkeley: University of California Press, 1977).

4. *High-Level Group on Administrative Burdens, Final Report on Administrative Burden Reduction,* July 24, 2014. http://ec.europa.eu/smart-regulation/refit/ admin_burden/high_level_group_en.htm.

5. http://www.bayern.de/politik/initiativen/ buerokratieabbau-und-deregulierung

6. German Constitutional Court decision [BVerfGE] 39, 1, 42; BVerfGE 53, 30, 57 f.; BVerfGE 77, 170, 214; BVerfGE 88, 203, 251; BVerfGE 90, 145, 195; BVerfGE 121, 317, 356 – settled case-law.

7. German Constitutional Court decision [BVerfGE] 81, 310 ff.; BVerfGE 84, 25 ff. – Konrad mineshaft (used as nuclear waste repository).

8. German Constitutional Court decision [BVerfGE] 104, 249 ff. – a nuclear power plant Biblis B.

9. See Peter M. Huber, "Bundesverfassungsrecht und Landesverfassungsrecht."

10. See German Constitutional Court decision [BVerfGE] 113, 273 ff.; Court of Justice of the European Union, judgment of February 26, 2013 (Case C-399/11) – Stefano Melloni.

11. See German Constitutional Court decision [BVerfGE] 112, 304, 320 – GPS surveillance; BVerfGE 114, 196, 247 – BSSG; Peter M. Huber, "Selbstverwaltung und Systemgerechtigkeit. Zu den Grenzen einer 'Professional-isierung' der Leitungsstrukturen Kassenärztlicher Vereinigungen" in *Vierteljahresschrift für Sozialrecht* [VSSR]

(2000), pp. 369/386 ff.; Peter Huber and Stefan Storr, *Wahltarife im SGB V* (Berlin: Duncker & Humblot, 2008), pp. 36 f.; Friedhelm Hufen, *Staatsrecht II, Grundrechte*, 4th edn., (Munich: C.H. Beck, 2014), § 8 n. 16; Jan Henrik Klement, "Die Kumulation von Grundrechtseingriffen im Umweltrecht" in *Archiv des oeffentlichen Rechts [AöR]* 134 (2009), pp. 35 ff.; Gregor Kirchhof, "Kumulative Belastung durch unterschiedliche staatliche Maßnahmen" in *Neue juristische Wochenschrift [NJW]* (2006), p. 732; Michael Kloepfer, "Belastungskumulationen durch Normenüberlagerungen im Abwasserrecht" in *Verwaltungsarchiv [VerwArch]* 74 (1983), pp. 201 ff.; Jörg Lücke, "Der additive Grundrechtseingriff sowie das Verbot der übermäßigen Gesamtbelastung des Bürgers," in *Deutsche Verwaltungsblatt [DVBl.]* (2001), pp. 1469 ff.

CHAPTER 8

CORPORATE SOCIAL RESPONSIBILITY AS A CORRECTIVE FORCE IN BUSINESS?

JÖRG ROCHOLL

I. INTRODUCTION

The international financial crisis that had begun by 2008 and that has continued in part until today has plunged our system of market economy into a serious legitimation crisis. Fundamental questions are being raised: does society profit from giving companies a "license to operate" in a free economic system? Or is it rather that companies exploit this opportunity to engage in activities that only help themselves while damaging society? At this point the usual critics start to complain that profits are increasingly privatized while losses are socialized. So how can we ensure that as well as taking responsibility for their own welfare, companies also assume responsibility towards society, and that they abstain from precisely those activities they know to be harmful to society?

In this discussion the theme of corporate social responsibility takes on a particular significance. Judged by the frequency with which this theme arises in public discussion, how often it is the subject of university curricula, and how intensively it is being researched, this topic is extremely popular at the moment. So let us now take a closer look at the notion of corporate social responsibility.

II. THE ORIGINS OF CORPORATE SOCIAL RESPONSIBILITY

Many of today's debates about corporate social responsibility follow from Milton Friedman's response to the question of what is the social responsibility of a company. Friedman said: "There is one and only one social responsibility of business—to use its resources and engage in activities designed to increase its profits..."[1] This definition is not in essence any different from a conventional description of corporate governance, as described by Shleifer and Vishny: "Corporate governance deals with the agency problem: the separation of management and finance. The fundamental question of corporate governance is how to assure financiers that they get a return on their financial investment."[2] According to this formulation corporate governance and corporate social responsibility should share the same aim, namely to maximize a company's profits and create high returns for its investors—a notion that, in this form, would enjoy little support today.

However Milton Friedman added a further qualification to his answer: *"...so long as it stays within the rules of the game,* which is to say, engages in open and free competition without deception or fraud."[3] Friedman consciously speaks not of laws but about "rules of the game," which include social norms and values as well as laws. Since the beginning of the financial crisis these rules of the game have altered. In my opinion three developments are responsible for this. What underpins all of them is that the general perception of the externalities arising from business activities has changed.

First, different investors have their own particular interests—as was the case even before 2007. Thus the interests of equity providers and debt capital providers do not always coincide. In particular equity providers, that is shareholders, can urge the management of a company to adopt strategies that would result in a transfer of assets from debt capital providers to equity providers by increasing the risk of the business undertaken, strategies that as a result are linked to externalities affecting debt capital providers. In economic terms, this is known as *agency cost of debt*. Debt capital providers try to rebalance this conflict using various means. So-called covenants in loan agreements are some of the best-known examples.

Second, externalities include other spheres. The actions of a company have consequences, not only for its investors but also for numerous other interest groups (also called stakeholders) or affected areas—its employees and the environment, for example. Here the concept of sustainability comes into play, which—even if it is used in the same sense as corporate social responsibility—clearly extends much further than the latter. Sustainability is not limited to the business world, but comprises all political and social projects that are intended to enable younger generations to continue using key resources. Here it is not just a question of actual externalities, but more about their public perception. Since as recently as the Brent Spar incident, but above all as a result of the significantly growing importance of social media, even alleged or minor infractions committed by a company against the rules of the game can lead to huge negative consequences. Companies are well aware of this fact. Indeed some observers claim that corporate social responsibility could replace the corrective forces that have disappeared as a result of increasing globalization and the decline in the importance of individual nation states.

Third—and perhaps most important for our purposes—the financial crisis has raised fundamental questions. In the case of the banks, especially, who because of their systemic relevance were classified as "too big/interconnected/complex to fail," externalities affecting taxpayers arose frequently and on a large scale. According to a 2012 OECD report actual creditor involvement took place in only four countries (Denmark, Iceland, Great Britain, and the USA) on more than one occasion, that is in the case of more than one failing bank. This means that as a rule creditors are not involved in what happens to banks and the financial system when they get into trouble—or if they are, then only to a limited extent. If they are involved at all, thus far they seem to have been involved only in the case of smaller banks; in the case of bigger banks they are overwhelmingly compensated by the state. The unity of ownership and liability that is fundamental to a market economy was thus infringed, and the legitimacy of a market-economy system was severely put to the test. To put it another way: such developments have placed a question mark over companies' "operating license," that is companies' license to operate, and perhaps even over the system of market economy itself.

Above all these three developments have resulted in the concept of corporate governance being understood today in a broader sense than before the start of the financial crisis. This is demonstrated in a document published by the European Commission, which has grappled with the consequences of the financial crisis for corporate governance in several Green Papers: "The traditional definition of corporate governance refers to relations between a company's senior management, its board of directors, its shareholders and other stakeholders, such as employees and their representatives. It also determines the structure used to define a company's objectives, as well as the means of achieving them and of monitoring the results obtained."[4]

III. WHAT ARE THE LIMITS OF CORPORATE SOCIAL RESPONSIBILITY?

These developments have also led to society expecting a sense of social responsibility from companies, particularly to a greater sensitivity in the question of which practices companies should undertake in order to increase profits, and from which they should refrain. This leads to the question of how far these social expectations should go. Here are three thoughts on this matter.

First, as a result of the financial crisis, numerous discussions have looked at the causes of corporate malpractice and how to eliminate them. Many of the empirical findings that emerged are not consistent with intuitively perceived patterns of behavior. Here it is worth looking at the most recent empirical findings. At first glance analyses of the relationship between corporate governance and the development of companies and banks during the financial crisis reveal something astonishing. Put simply we can summarize it as follows: elements of corporate governance that were frequently described before the crisis as sustainable and important, such as better shareholder representation, were of no help during the crisis. On the contrary they were even sometimes associated with a worse business performance. Thus studies show that companies with independent boards and a high proportion of institutional investors, who should have been better informed than retail investors, registered worse share returns than other companies. This finding leads to the conclusion that these same companies assumed high risks before the start of the crisis. Similarly, banks with shareholder-friendly boards performed worse during the crisis than other banks. Another central finding was that banks in countries with strict capital requirements and independent regulators performed better. Therefore what is important is the general regulatory environment in which the banks operate, not the corporate governance of the individual bank.

Another study shows that during the crisis banks did not perform better if the interests of their CEOs, through their shares and equity-related compensation packages, seemed to correspond with the interests of their companies. Some findings reveal that these banks even performed worse. Finally, a study shows that the extent of risky business practices in banks is linked positively to the relative power of shareholders in the corporate governance of these banks.

These findings suggest that the independence of boards was not much help during the crisis, or was even a hindrance. It may well be that independent board members compared the performance of their own bank with the supposedly better performance of other banks, and thus inquired less (or wanted to inquire less) into the risks being taken. The resulting pressure on their management could have been counterproductive if, as a result of this pressure, the management took more risks that were not in the best interests of the company in the long term. In any case, these observations and empirical findings show that supposed panaceas such as independence are not as straightforward as was frequently assumed—before the crisis in particular. This ambiguous empirical evidence should give us food for thought when offering companies suggestions for improvement that only seem obvious, and when developing specific expectations of them.

But on the topic of corporate social responsibility there is also a second question: who actually decides what a company's social responsibility should look like, and how and where it should involve itself? To put it another way: in a democratic society, should the definition of what is socially desirable not come from legislators? An important example of this is the consideration of how companies should deal with current tax legislation. Should they simply pay those taxes that are demanded by statute or more, ignoring legal loopholes or special circumstances? That is, should they bear a tax burden that is also socially determined and morally desirable beyond what is demanded by statute? We can hardly expect the latter, as this would make companies open to attack from their investors.

There is also a third and final point. If one tries to refine and concretize expectations of corporate social responsibility more and more, the belief might arise that everything is allowed that is not explicitly forbidden. This could result in an unnecessary amount of bureaucracy, publishing voluminous company reports on its own activities in the area of corporate social responsibility, and "ticking boxes," and thus elevating form over content. Such excesses would no longer have anything to do with improving the situation, but would merely lead to improved compliance on paper.

IV. CONCLUSIONS

Corporate social responsibility is a highly pertinent topic that demands intensive academic and regulatory discussion. The financial crisis itself has subjected the corporate "license to operate" and the market-economic system to a serious examination by society. Thus it is clear and logical that companies must meet the challenges of rendering their activities transparent, making themselves publicly accountable, exercising restraint, and refraining from doing anything that damages society—with the aim of building trust.

However, academic studies also show that it is often not easy to issue concrete recommendations for action that apply at all times and in all contexts. The empirical evidence is not always as clear as is generally expected—sometimes it is even counter-intuitive. The demand for corporate social responsibility should thus be formulated with care; and corporate social responsibility certainly cannot be the panacea for solving the problems of society.

Notes

1. Milton Friedman, *New York Times Magazine*, September 13, 1970.
2. Andrei Shleifer, Robert W. *Vishny, The Journal of Finance*, 1997, 52, p. 773.
3. Friedman, *New York Times Magazine*.
4. European Commission, Green Paper, *EU development policy in support of inclusive growth and sustainable development*, Brussels, 2010a.

CHAPTER 9

GIVE UP GROWTH?

KAI A. KONRAD

Should economies in the developed world give up
economic growth? Is the growth of gross domestic
product merely an idol to which industrialized societies under the influence of the West pay homage? A
starting point for the critique of growth lies in the
deliberations of the Club of Rome and its 1972 report
The Limits to Growth, as well as in debates in the area
of resource economics. Planet Earth is endowed with
a finite supply of depletable natural resources. Envi-
ronmentalists highlight the dangers of global warming if growth and the unfettered emission of green-

house gases continue.[1] And research into happiness also reveals findings that are skeptical of growth: when it comes to human happiness growth in material prosperity seems less important. Research has shown that there exists no clear, at any rate no linear connection between a society's material prosperity and the extent of "happiness" reported by the population, although at an individual level a boost in income does produce an effect.[2]

In politics, these ideas resonate most strongly in an environment where economic growth is weak. Former French President Nicolas Sarkozy set up a group of social scientists led by Nobel Prize winner Joseph E. Stiglitz, Amartya Sen, and Harvard professor Jean-Paul Fitoussi to investigate the measurement of well-being. In their final report from 2009 they discuss the problems involved in measuring prosperity.[3] In Germany the commission on "Wachstum, Wohlstand, Lebensqualität—Wege zu nachhaltigem Wirtschaften und gesellschaftlichem Fortschritt in der Sozialen Marktwirtschaft" reported to the German Bundestag.[4] This report too can be seen within the debate as a critique of economic policy that exclusively or predominantly pursues growth.[5]

Many economists are greatly concerned by these trends towards the critique of growth. They point out that the momentum of economic growth offers people individual opportunities for social mobility. They also point out that without growth many social problems and problems associated with the welfare state will be almost impossible to manage. In this context the increasing aging of our society and the rise in public debt are particularly important.

Much has already been said and written about the controversy surrounding the idea of giving up economic growth so I shall not repeat it here.[6] In this essay I will be addressing only two aspects. From the individual perspective, giving up growth proves to be a rather unlikely option. And that may be good, as global economic growth proves to offer an important answer to some global challenges.

THE INDIVIDUAL PERSPECTIVE

In his analysis of the social limits to growth, Fred Hirsch[7] described how an increase in a society's material wealth cannot lead to a similar rise in everyone's prosperity. He points out that the number of managerial positions in a society is to a great extent independent of its material prosperity. Insofar as human desires focus on status, prestige, or other advantages that accompany the achievement of outstanding social positions, the material growth of a society is of little help: they cannot increase the number of these work positions that are scarce in some absolute sense. Robert Frank[8] has devoted most of his academic work to the topic of status, and has expanded upon Hirsch's ideas. Economic prosperity often focuses on the possession or use of goods that are few and non-renewable in number. They remain limited in terms of quantity, even if economic power grows considerably. Our society may increase its per capita income one hundred-fold, but the number of outstanding works of art from the Impressionist period or the number of works by Leonardo da Vinci will not increase by one single item. In this generally richer society the most exquisite works of art and the most attractive of the other non-renewable goods will also be owned by society's richest members. In a society that is one hundred times richer, a middle-class person who earns an annual salary of four million euros instead of 40,000 euros will still not become the owner of really outstanding works of art, or of the most sought-after property. In this respect it is one of the fundamental experiences of our society to which Robert Frank refers: relative wealth buys goods that are scarce in some absolute sense.

This issue may go some way to explain why the happiness of a representative member of a society does not increase proportionately with the general level of income. We might also conclude from this that increasing material wealth fails to deliver on its promises. The increase in the prosperity of the individual in an otherwise unchanged society produces benefits for this person which do not come about if the whole of society becomes correspondingly richer. Individual striving for material prosperity that exceeds the prosperity of others creates a growth dynamic and a great accumulation of wealth. At the same time the increase in wellbeing sought by the individual fails to materialize.[9]

This issue and its accompanying frustration may contribute to the prevailing skepticism about growth. If the whole of society were to give up their striving for more, each individual member would not be worse off in social terms, but everyone would save a lot of energy. The idea of collectively renouncing the notion of status or of directing status-based thinking away from material prosperity and towards socially acceptable behavior or spiritual matters has a certain intellectual appeal. This is particularly applicable to members of a society whose income has allowed them to penetrate areas where the basic material needs for food, clothing, shelter, etc., have become secondary.

The chances of realizing this departure from status-based thinking are not good. It is likely that the reasons for this are rooted deep in human nature. Even in a society where growth has been collectively slowed down the really essential problems of distribution remain, namely the conflicts of distribution surrounding the commodities that are scarce in some absolute sense—and that Frank calls "positional" goods. In this scenario, the individual need for a higher income, to climb higher on the ladder of wealth and assets, is often purely instrumental. For example, it is hard to imagine society without conflicts about the most desirable male or female partner. In this existential situation who would not try to pursue their individual goals?

It may be regrettable, but in the modern societies I am acquainted with conflict about one's dream partner plays a considerable role in the flaunting of status goods. Of course the right car cannot replace a charming personality and a handsome outward appearance. However, a Porsche or a Ferrari, in combination with a winning smile, can provide a lot of additional persuasion. The biological foundations of our existence may also be the force behind the fact that the economic and financial circumstances of a male or female candidate can play a significant role in the choice of partner. Research into marriage carried out by Lena Edlund, for example, provides models that explain our choice of human partnerships in the past, present, and future.[10]

Status-related consumption is an almost ubiquitous phenomenon. Unlike food or clothing, the advantage derived from the consumption of status-related goods derives from social context. With this type of consumption the consumer is indirectly pursuing other goals. Often he wants to tell others about certain issues: his wealth, his good taste, his membership of a certain status group, etc. Ultimately, these characteristics help to attain what the consumer considers to be actually desirable, which includes recognition and esteem from his desired partner.

Status-related consumption, which is oriented towards economic wealth, is not an invention of modern capitalist consumer society. It is a widespread mode of behavior in which economic purchasing power makes use of renewable resources in order to distinguish oneself from others. Even in the so-called socialist societies of the 20th century, where material equality is one of the central objective variables in politics, status goods and status symbols play an important role.

As a skeptic of growth one can cherish the hope of a society where the distribution of goods that are scarce in some absolute sense is not effected by means of relative wealth, with the result that a majority of the incentives for increasing one's individual prosperity are neutralized. The chance of that happening seems implausible, and rightly so. The dynamics of growth that results from this distribution competition has a very positive side effect which I will describe now.

THE GLOBAL PERSPECTIVE

"Spaceship Earth," the home of human civilization, is a fragile thing. Making people aware of this was a major cognitive achievement. It can be attributed to various developments, not least of which was space travel, which gave us the first image of the "blue planet" as it moves unprotected through the vast universe. The politics of climate change and awareness of the significance of a possible global climate catastrophe may be a result of this revelation. The increase in knowledge about the history and presumed future of our solar system, as well as about the role of the various protection systems that make life on Earth possible, demonstrate the fragile foundations of human life on this planet. They make us aware of the multiple possible dangers that emphasize the current threat of climate catastrophe.

The economist and Nobel Prize winner Thomas C. Schelling[11] has highlighted an important issue regarding the threatening consequences of climate change. Schelling's formula recommends the greatest possible "adaptability" of economy and society. By this he means the capability and possibility of adapting to these life circumstances and of surviving, or rather enabling a good life under these changed conditions. A high degree of adaptability is based on three related economic and social situations. First we would need the greatest possible technological apparatus to shield us successfully against the dangerous effects of global changes and to exploit the opportunities that arise from such changes. Such a collection of formulae and blueprints is useless if two further conditions are not fulfilled. Society must have widespread access to the know-how that reveals which blueprints have already been researched and how these can be implemented and applied. And we must have the economic potential in terms of resources and production capacity to deploy the technologies that are available and that are considered suitable. Adaptability is a function of research, education, and material prosperity.

Schelling's ideas should have even more validity when we consider how we deal with other major risks. They refer to a fundamental conflict. On the one hand by giving up research and educational investment, and by giving up major production potential, it may be possible to suspend or slow down individual processes through which people change their own environment, for example climate change, the central topic of Schelling's discussion. At the same time, giving this up also means giving up the ability to react appropriately to unavoidable and largely unforeseen changes in the environment. As I understand his argument, Schelling attributes particular importance to adaptability in the face of the unpredictability of possible changes.

SUMMARY

To summarize: status-based consumption and the striving for relative economic prosperity lead unavoidably to frustration from an individual perspective. This may contribute to an increasing skepticism towards growth in society. From a global perspective, however, a dynamic economy creates an important side effect. Only a technologically progressive, well-educated, and preferably affluent population can react with sufficient flexibility to catastrophes and changes in living conditions.

Notes

1. Cf. on estimations of danger and suggestions for solutions, e.g. IPPC Fifth Assessment Report, "Climate Change 2014."

2. Joachim Weimann, Andreas Knabe, and Ronnie Schöb, *Geld macht doch glücklich, Wo die ökonomische Glücksforschung irrt* (Stuttgart: Schäffer und Poeschel, 2012).

3. This report titled "Measurement of Economic Performance and Social Progress" reveals the tension between a commitment to an improved measurement of objective indicators, including income, assets, consumption, etc., on the one hand, and subjective indicators of wellbeing on the other. The theses central to the opposition to growth, however, do not add any fuel to this report.

4. Concluding report of the German Bundestag's inquiry "Wachstum, Wohlstand, Lebensqualität—Wege zu nachhaltigem Wirtschaften und gesellschaftlichem Fortschritt in der Sozialen Marktwirtschaft." German Bundestag publication 17/13300, 17. Parliamentary term 03.05.2013

5. In fact in its multiplicity of dissenting opinions the report reveals a large plurality of notions and assessments that reflect the controversy about growth in politics and society.

6. Cf. for example Meinhard Miegel, *Exit, Wohlstand ohne Wachstum, Bundeszentrale für politische Bildung* (Bonn: Bundeszentrale für politische Bildung, 2010) and Karl-Heinz Paque, "Warum Wachstum? Sechs gute Gründe für eine gute Sache," in Initiative Neue Soziale Marktwirtschaft

(ed.), *Die Wohlstandsfrage—6 Visionen für nachhaltiges Wachstum* (Berlin: INSM, 2012), pp. 37–53.

7. Fred Hirsch, *Social Limits to Growth* (Cambridge, Mass.: Harvard University Press, 1976).

8. Robert Frank, *Choosing the Right Pond: Human Behaviour and the Quest for Status* (Oxford: Oxford University Press, 1988).

9. Cf. on the consequences for capital accumulation and the distribution of assets that result from status preferences focused on relative wealth, Kai A. Konrad, "Relative Wealth Reconsidered" in *Journal of Economic Behavior & Organization*, 18 (2), (1992), pp. 215–27.

10. Lena Edlund, "Marriage: Past, Present, Future?" in *CESifo Economic Studies*, 52 (4), (2006), pp. 621–39.

11. Thomas C. Schelling, "Some Economics of Global Warming" in *American Economic Review*, 82 (1), (1992), pp. 1–14.

CHAPTER 10

ELOQUENT SILENCE AND ACTING THROUGH INACTION: ON THE MEANING OF CALMNESS

PIRMIN STEKELER-WEITHOFER

There exist logically "flat" opinions concerning the relationship between action and inaction. They suggest a simple *symmetry* of mere *negation*. In this an inaction is simply the non-execution of an action, while an action seems simply to be the omission of inaction. This case would thus be reconstructed in the same way as a case wherein something is called big if one can negate that it is small, and similarly a small thing is the negation of the big. But already the fact that light or brightness is not simply the absence of darkness shows, as seen incidentally by Heraclitus (the philosopher who was only allegedly obscure), that some cases are *not* symmetrical: darkness is indeed the absence of light, or metaphorically, of clarity. The reverse, however, is false. Light is not the absence of darkness; the communicated clarity of a speech is not the absence of obscure formulations. Similarly the true is also not simply the absence of the incorrect. The refutation of something false is often not enough upon which to base a truth.

Let us look at a very old example. The sentence "Peter stopped beating his wife" can be false in the normal, finite sense if Peter was still beating his wife. The sentence is or can be called false in the infinite sense if he never beat her. Similarly a sentence such as "Caesar is not a prime number" can be seen as the infinite negation or refutation of a logical category mistake. Since Parmenides, Socrates, Plato, and Aristotle this insight lies at the heart of a logical critique of formalist sophists and sophisms, even if it is constantly forgotten most recently in the work of Frege, Russell, and the young Wittgenstein. For the time being and for our purposes only this key sentence is important: silence is not simply not-speaking. Inaction is not simply an omission.

In a book on the subject of "action and inaction," however, my colleague from Düsseldorf, Professor Dieter Birnbacher, has advanced a modified theory of symmetry.[1] For example, if the moral rightness of an action would qualify as nothing other than the rightness of the corresponding not-doing, simply with regard to the expected good results or consequences, then one would indeed have to value doing and not-doing as symmetrical. Indeed this is precisely what ethical utilitarianism as moral consequentialism seems to do. On the other hand we should bear in mind that in our legal systems we distribute responsibilities differently. In France and Germany there exists the special case of the criminal offense of the omission to rescue [unterlassene Hilfeleistung] even with regard to strangers (although ultimately it is usually just a question of fetching help or informing the police). In the USA, however, there is no such legal duty in practice, no "duty to rescue," except in special cases such as parents' care of their children or the duty of care of one's superiors. One is not legally obliged to help a "stranger" who is in life-threatening danger, even if this is supposedly "morally" necessary. In legal terms such assistance is supererogatory, in the ghastly jargon for an action that does more good than is necessary (legally and perhaps also morally). In supererogatory actions, legal or moral duties are exceeded. In much that we consider morally good legal duties are exceeded. It would be wrong to change this by making everything that is morally good into a legal duty.

So how can we understand the asymmetries between doing and not-doing, asymmetries that are at least imaginable and perhaps even obvious? Returning to the example of *silence*, great philosophers such as Laozi, Buddha, Meister Eckhart, or even Martin Heidegger, together with a large group of religious and philosophical mystics that followed them, demonstrated that *silence* and *calmness* [*Gelassenheit*; also translated as *releasement* in Heidegger] are highly complex intentional *actions*.

More precisely, calmness is the correct *attitude* [*Haltung*] to the contingencies of our life in particular, and the correct way of *going about* [*Umgang*] a wide range of all kinds of unpredictable events. With difficulty we must adopt such attitudes and such a way of life by recognizing and acknowledging the limits of our pre-science and ability to act.

Silence and calmness consciously negate active interventions that are often also expressively and declaratively obvious, positive actions, and opt for inaction. In such cases, silence or not-doing are certainly examples of an action as well. They are an action in a far more extreme sense than an immediate verbal reaction or a rash act that wants to maintain control over things. These responses are found in the many social processes involved in the practical recognition or non-recognition of systems, even when such responses are meaningless, and in the end disoriented and not carefully targeted.

Of course inaction is not always more challenging than action, and never in the literal or trivial sense of merely doing nothing. It is, however, in the first place always part of the framework for evaluating every action. Thus it belongs, as philosophers like to say, to the a priori assumptions and transcendental conditions of every act. Second, in cases where certain typical reactions or actions are obvious, it is often very difficult to resist the temptation to intervene through actions or even just words, and leave things to take their course, instead of subjugating these things to one's own will or keeping them under one's own power and control. This is often far better than any well-intentioned action.

The importance of this general insight into the preference for inaction, particularly in questions of legal, social, and peace policy, can be seen in the following gnomic mnemonic from Laozi's *Tao Te Ching*:

> The best leaders are those their people hardly know
> exist.
> The next best is a leader who is loved and praised.
> Next comes the one who is feared.
> The worst one is the leader that is despised...
> The best leaders value their words, and use them spar-
> ingly.
> When they have accomplished their task,
> the people say, "Amazing!
> We did it, all by ourselves!"

This quotation is clearly still politically controversial today, especially as it directly rejects any accusation of "sitting out" problems. Nevertheless one problem is that the space of not-doing is much bigger than the space of actively doing something specific. Furthermore both "spaces" are in the first place spaces of mere opportunity. In what way do they exist at all, as one cannot see mere opportunities? And why do we always evaluate an actualized action or inaction with a view to possible alternatives, and never merely with a view to the actual action and its actual consequences alone? So why and how do we evaluate an action always by comparison with an inaction or with some other kind of action?

In this Hegel recognizes the central principle of reason for any institutional change and any suggestion for the development of the sciences. It is the *constructive vote of no confidence*. This states that a given political, legal, social, or even merely conceptual system (in the implicit, empractic use of language and in mnemonics and forms of inference of theoretically canonized knowledge) can only be changed in a rational way if one knows in advance that the new systems might solve the general problems of good communication and cooperation better than the previous ones. Thus it must be shown first, that the new system can do more than the old system, both intrinsically and realistically; and second, that the costs of attaining the new system are not greater than the not merely hoped for but secured "additional benefit" of the new system.

It seems to me that over the last 200 years Germany has become a country that does not comprehend its greatest thinkers. People do not understand that Hegel's praise for the Reformation and with it the development of institutions through proposals for reform, which filter slowly into collective recognition after long debates, are balanced by the critique of a purely Utopian revolution, as seen for example in Robespierre's France.

Exactly 100 years after 1914, an analysis of the causes of our century's most elemental tragedy reveals the following structural facts: the catastrophe was clearly the consequence of proactive action on the part of the Central Powers. This resulted from an all-too-obvious reaction against being apparently surrounded by France and Russia. Nevertheless the pre-emptive war, particularly against France, was certainly not a "world power grab," as historian Fritz Fischer argued persuasively in his book *Griff nach der Weltmacht. Die Kriegzielpolitik des kaiserlichen Deutschland 1914–1918.*[2] Nevertheless the attack on Belgium while advancing towards France is a record of the impatient desire to hold on to the law of military action, and thus in view of the political situation meant more than a slight lack of calmness.

The German love of action in political *movements*—from the *Burschenschaften* [student fraternities] at the Wartburg Festival and later student movements, via the Nazis, to all left-wing movements after 1968—leads Germany as a whole into a kind of hyperactive state of permanent political revolution that persists today, although now represented as small-scale revolutions.

This general problem can be seen very clearly in the policies affecting German schools and universities. The G8 system reform, dealing with the alignment of school systems according to international standards that require 12 years of schooling before university admission, was introduced into high schools and then abolished again. University reforms

incorporating modular and tiered BA and MA programs were introduced and then immediately par-
tially abolished via the retention of a state examination for high-school teachers. Higher Education
Autonomy Acts, in the form of laws restricting the
freedom of university teachers, were introduced and
then abolished. Elsewhere a kind of frantic stasis pre-
vails, particularly in the sciences, instead of a calm
approach to work in a not entirely catastrophic postwar system.

The real irritation in Germany is not the perpetual
complaints of the postwar generation and baby-
boomers, who have done particularly well in terms
of prosperity and the law. What is irritating is that
these complaints are given credence, alongside the
busybodying that goes with them. This is turned into
a kind of permanent revolution where no one deals
calmly with his own past, present and future anymore. Ultimately everyone is confused and still wants
to save the world. However, the omission to act to
help a world that wants to be happy in a non-German
(i.e. non-know-it-all) kind of way is not a moral error.
It is much more a virtue of calmness that is restricted
to the immediate vicinity of one's own country, rather
than being extended to the *jardin* that *il faut cultiver*.

A dramatic example can be seen in the current debate about so-called assisted suicide, as demonstrated convincingly, in my opinion, in an article by Harald Wohlrapp.[3] In the article Wohlrapp argues forcefully for the rethinking of an assumption which, as he says, is taken for granted in the whole debate about the legal approval of assisting someone to kill themselves on request and about the moral defense of suicide, namely that that "freedom of choice in dying may represent an increase in the individual's freedom of self-determination."

It is a textbook example of philosophical logic to show why this can be or is an illusion. Wohlrapp cites a striking example from a Dutch case, in which a seriously ill woman complains about her ailments and is told: "But that is your choice." The dialectic works as follows. In a situation where we do *not* regard suicides in general as good responses to suffering but make them a taboo subject as a fundamentally morally problematic attitude—as supposedly enlightened people do—and thus at best show understanding for the "suicide" in regrettable exceptional cases, the individual does not have to decide to carry on living. He most certainly does not have to justify this decision. If we change this situation in our moral judgment or even within our legal system, then not committing suicide becomes an action that one has to justify to oneself and to others. Wilhelm Kamlah creates an entire philosophical anthropology to explain his later suicide as morally legitimate in light of his suffering—in spite of the foreseeable consequences for his family.[4] In my judgment such a revision of traditional morality is impossible. There can be no *general* ethical justification for suicide, no list of general test conditions which, if fulfilled, means that we not only regrettably understand suicide in the same way as we see any killing or some war as regrettably unavoidable, but that we even morally respect the person.

It could be that thinking along the lines of moral "taboos" and "prejudices" was more rational than we might suspect today, and more than the recent revisionist systems of morality lead us to believe. In any case these systems run the risk of succumbing to the extremely subjective and at the same time proof-based hyperactive illusion that any given standard or form of practice must be accounted for to us and to me each time in a new and convincing way, and if it is not, that it is invalid for us or for me. According to Hegel, even Kant fell victim to this illusion of an all-too radical "enlightenment" of simply "thinking for oneself," and all Kantians with him, as I try to show in my reading of Hegel's *Phenomenology of Spirit*, one of the most important philosophical works of all time.[5]

Moreover the saying "I'll go when life is only suffering" comes dangerously close to the saying "après moi, le déluge." In a similar attitude of utilitarian consequentialism it would be correspondingly wrong not to kill oneself or to allow oneself to be killed under certain circumstances, for example if one's own suffering and the burden upon relatives, the community, or even just on an insurance company brings more unhappiness or suffering as a whole into the world than a quick death. The proximity of this idea to the Nazi notions of eradicating "vermin harmful to the people" and "superfluous eaters" should be obvious, even if our somewhat saccharine era does not like to be reminded of such memories.

Notes

1. Dieter Birnbacher, *Tun und Unterlassen* (Stuttgart: Reclam, 1995); ibid., "Sterbehilfe—eine philosophische Sicht" in Felix Thiele (ed.), *Aktive und Passive Sterbehilfe. Medizinische, rechtswissenschaftliche und philosophische Aspekte* (Munich: Fink, 2010), pp. 31–42.

2. English translation: *Germany's Aims in the First World War* (New York: W.W. Norton, 1968).

3. Harald Wohlrapp, "Nachdenken über Sterbehilfe" in

Wissenswert. Online-Journal der Universität Hamburg, 3rd edn., 2014.

4. Wilhelm Kamlah, *Philosophische Anthropologie. Sprachkritische Grundlegung und Ethik* (Mannheim: Bibliografisches Institut, 1973). See also Geert-Lueke Lueken, "Ethik als philosophische Anthropologie. Zur Verteidigung des Kamlah-Projekts" in Jürgen Mittelstraß (ed.), *Der Konstruktivismus in der Philosophie im Ausgang von Wilhelm Kamlah und Paul Lorenzen* (Paderborn: Mentis, 2008), pp. 155–66; Pirmin Stekeler-Weithofer, "Ethik und politische Anthropologie" in Mittelstraß (ed.), *Der* Konstruktivismus, pp. 133–54.

5. Pirmin Stekeler-Weithofer, *Hegels Phänomenologie des Geistes*, 2 vols., (Hamburg: Meiner, 2014).

CHAPTER 11

THE CHOICES OF OMITTING AND REFRAINING IN THE VISUAL ARTS

GERT-RUDOLF FLICK

Art always implies an activity without which no art could be created. However there are various degrees to which the resources at one's disposal can or should be applied. The artist has the option to omit some resources, consciously to refrain from using all resources at once.

In this context we are discussing the principle of "less is more" or rather, perhaps, "less could be more." Over time artists have made great progress in their search for perfection, for example the introduction of perspective, the treatment of shadows, and suchlike. In Raphael's work, this development led to a kind of perfection that was almost unsurpassable. Raphael's followers such as Giulio Romano were at a loss: now what was one to do since one's predecessor had already produced a kind of perfection that could not be surpassed? In order to create something really new, the only solution was to give up the search for perfection and intentionally create works of art that contradicted the rules of perfection. This is the starting point of Mannerism which followed Raphael's High Renaissance style. Of course the abandonment of perfection was an act of conscious not-doing, driven by the desire to find a distinct style and to differentiate oneself from Raphael's perfectionism. If the Mannerists were ultimately unsuccessful, the reasons were twofold. There was among their number no painter who compared to Raphael; and the advent of the Counter-Reformation brought about militant demands for a return to realistic perfection.

In any case the way in which Raphael was received is extremely important for the theme of restraint in art. Among the three great artists of the High Renaissance—Leonardo, Michelangelo and Raphael—it was only Raphael's posthumous fame that was subject to substantial fluctuations. In the 17th century, in the

Baroque period, Raphael was valued much less highly than Michelangelo, and this evaluation still prevailed even in the 18th century. Raphael's ratings rose once more in the 19th century, only to fall again in the modern era.

Objections to Raphael lay most of all in the perfection he had achieved. A perfect work of art lays a kind of trap for the viewer from which he cannot extricate himself easily. On the one hand, he cannot fail to admire such perfection, but the viewer does not come only to express his admiration—this would quickly tire him. The viewer secretly wants to enter into a kind of dialogue with the art work, but here perfection is obstructive—as strange as that may sound. A perfect art work admits of no dialogue, as it cuts off any debate about a possible alternative approach. But a not-quite-perfect work of art is something quite different. It stimulates the viewer's imagination and allows the art work a bit of mysteriousness or mystique which does the viewer's soul good. For example, over the centuries people have debated whether Leonardo's *Mona Lisa* is laughing, smiling, or merely gazing amusedly out from the picture. This is precisely what a good work of art should do: it should have a bit of mystery.

In the fine arts the full application of all pictorial resources leads ultimately to a result that is not completely satisfying. Therefore some of these resources must be omitted so that the art work can maintain its mystique. In the field of fine art we can even talk about a commandment of not-doing, that is not applying all available resources. Great artists have always understood how to strike the right balance in this context.

Perhaps one example of this notion is the attraction of primitive art. I am thinking here of the prehistorical art of the Cyclades, of the Iberians, even of early medieval sculptures, or Italian painting before Giotto. Since Vasari these forms of artistic expression have long been considered of little interest, as the artists of the time only applied limited amounts of artistic resources. It can remain open whether this was a result of conscious actions or whether the artists were actually incapable of performing better. The fact is that these art works are not perfect, and for a long time this was considered a minus point among the artistic community who were trained to appreciate perfection. Today, however, this situation has reversed. Primitive art is accorded a high value once more precisely because it concentrates on the essentials, thereby producing a powerful, clear statement.

Picasso, Brancusi, Modigliani, and others have been fundamentally influenced by primitive art. And what these artists found attractive in primitive art was precisely the refusal to apply all resources.

It is historically interesting to see which cultural artifacts were looted from conquered nations by their conquerors. Let us take the example of Napoleon's art theft from Germany. The commissioner charged with this task, Baron Vivant Denon, seized from Germany mainly primitive art, in which he included pre-Renaissance painting. He said: "In these paintings there exists such pure originality, such a moving naivety, such an authentic expression, such a simplicity, and such a deep faith that I prefer them to the works of most of our great artists who do nothing more than copy each other."

It is interesting that this statement should emerge from the lips of the very same Vivant Denon who in his role as French cultural minister was responsible for the Academy's increasingly boring glorification of Napoleon. Vivant Denon understood that heroic images of Napoleon, which were perfect in the technical application of all resources, ultimately left the viewer cold, as they ran counter to the principle of "less is more." Primitive art, by contrast, was refreshingly different. It is to Vivant Denon's credit that he had the wit to look beyond his own cultural and political horizons, despite all his governmental tasks.

Another example is the decline of the art academies and of academic painting in particular. For centuries the aim of drawing lessons at the academies was to render sculptures or models as precisely as possible, that is to attain a high level of perfection. Around 1860 this had led to perfect but scarcely nuanced history paintings and heroic portraits. As one artist would imitate another in the search for perfection, the output became more and more interchangeable and it was increasingly hard to distinguish between them. The desire for perfection had led to a uniform and ultimately sterile kind of painting. Then Manet suddenly appeared on the scene, suppressing shadows and locating his characters in spaces that were not organized according to perspective. He put a lot of effort into painting some parts of his pictures, but neglected others that were less important to him. Initially the outcry was huge, and Manet had difficulties exhibiting at the Salon. Over time, however, the public began to enjoy his pictures. Here, once again, we see the principle of "less is more" in operation. Using this principle Manet and the Impressionists who came after him outperformed academic art between

1880 and 1910, and created the foundation for modern painting.

However it is not the case that the principle of "less is more" was always acknowledged or validated in art history. During Rembrandt's career it even entailed catastrophic consequences. At first Rembrandt enjoyed great success as a portrait painter. However, when he began to turn his attention to the essential element of a commissioned portrait, namely the face, and only painted his patron's clothing in a sketchy way, many customers turned away. In their opinion, for the price they were paying they could demand a painting that was fully painted in every detail. Rembrandt refused to adapt his style to the required standards, and as a result was given fewer and fewer commissions, finally going bankrupt.

In the modern period the omission of possible resources was consciously pursued. Using just a few pictorial means abstract painting achieved astonishing results, and speaks to large swathes of the population precisely because of this. Indeed the decision not to apply resources has become an essential indicator of modernity, with the result that perhaps one can speak of the art of inaction. Modern artists have made "less is more" their motto, and in doing so have enjoyed great success.

The desire to reduce the possible means of expression, and thus also the possible forms of expression, had already been espoused by the Russian painters Wassily Kandinsky and Kasimir Malevich before and during World War I. Malevich's *Black Square* on a white background is a simplification and reduction of painterly resources, which until then had been considered impossible. In 1960s New York this view of things was taken up by a new generation of painters and led to an art movement called Minimalism. Outstanding exponents of this trend were Frank Stella, Kenneth Noland, Ellsworth Kelly, Piet Mondrian, and Yves Klein. Barnett Newman, Ad Reinhardt, and Josef Albers were also influenced by Minimalism. Ad Reinhardt expressed his understanding of it in this way: "The more stuff in it, the busier the work of art, the worse it is. More is less. Less is More. The eye is a menace to clear sight. The laying bare of oneself is obscene. Art begins with the getting rid of nature." He could hardly express the principle of "less is more" any more clearly, although Reinhardt was also referring to the corresponding principle of "more is less." If more is less then less itself is something more, as the viewer can complete the less using his own imagination. This is precisely the reason Minimalism is popular in our era, and will remain so for the time being.

Minimalism is not only pertinent in the work of painters. Sculptors or object-makers such as Donald Judd and Dan Flavin created minimalistic objects, with Donald Judd consciously drawing on the clarity and simplicity of American folk art.

Minimalism has also been applied to architecture, primarily under the influence of Mies van der Rohe, who organized the essential elements of a building in such a way as to create the impression of extreme simplicity. The use of geometric forms and their conscious repetition, simple materials such as glass, concrete, and steel, the rejection of ornamentation, and the use of natural light gave the impression of truth to materials on the one hand, and on the other led to a perception of order and intrinsic characteristics. Modern architects such as Tadao Ando and Peter Zumthor draw explicitly on the philosophy of Mies van der Rohe.

However it would be unjust to celebrate the principle of "less is more" exclusively as an achievement of Western culture. The notion of applying painterly resources sparingly in order to heighten the effect appears in many cultures, particularly in the ancient culture of Zen. In Japanese Zen philosophy the sparse use of resources and simplicity of form is not only an aesthetic value but also a moral imperative to acknowledge the essence of nature and to investigate materials and objects through their inner qualities. Such research would then lead to the freedom and essence of being. One aesthetic principle in Zen philosophy is the principle of *ma*, the creation of empty, open spaces, and the removal of all walls dividing outside from inside. Another principle is called *wabi-sabi*, that is the elimination of all unnecessary elements in an object, for example a flower. In the Japanese art of flower arranging, or *ikebana*, twigs, leaves, and roots are cut away so that only the essential parts of the flower remain. In this way the essence of the flower and its inner character are made visible.

Thus "less is more" is recognized not only in Western art as a generally valid principle in fine art, as on the one hand it makes it easier for the viewer to recognize the essence of things, and on the other it enables the viewer to participate over and above the experience of mere admiration. Only the non-application of all artistic resources can bring about a dialogue with the viewer, enabling the latter to add something from his imagination. This triggers a deep sense of inner satisfaction in the viewer and connects him to the work of art, beyond the brief moment of a snapshot.

CHAPTER 12

THE TEN COMMANDMENTS YESTERDAY AND TODAY: TOWARDS A FOUNDATION FOR ACTING JUSTLY

FRIEDHELM MENNEKES

Every society must commit to a system of institutions and patterns of action if it wants to stand the test of time. In ancient times such systems were established by rulers and then constituted detailed information for the individual, giving him direction and instruction for everyday life, while at the same time stabilizing the social system. In this way the whole of society was taken into account by law and justice, while at the same time institutions legitimized their dominance once more. As basic notions of morality have both sociological and anthropological foundations, it comes as no surprise that they are similar, both in the early advanced civilizations of the ancient East, and in the territories of Mesopotamia and Egypt. Everywhere the task was to build a society and secure the welfare of the people. It was the same in ancient Israel. Here, too, we find the notions and laws that determine the lives of the people, and of their tribes, the lives of the individuals in the middle of society and those on the periphery, the widows and orphans, the children and the poor. On closer examination we can see the centrality accorded to the idea of not-doing.

ORIGINS IN MYTH AND RELIGION

The beginnings were documented early on by Ur-Nammu, founder of the Third Dynasty of Ur (2112–2095 BCE). At the very start of his reign he sets out the following regulation as one of the aims of his laws: "The orphan was not delivered up to the rich man; the widow was not delivered up to the mighty man; the man of one shekel was not delivered up to the man of one mina."[1]

Shortly before 1786 BCE, in the epilogue to his famous codex, Hammurabi of Babylon explains that the law is there for everyone to depend upon when he speaks of his personal desire for justice for every individual: "In my breast I cherish the inhabitants of the land of Sumer and Akkad; in my shelter I have let them repose in peace; in my deep wisdom have I enclosed them. That the strong might not injure the weak, in order to protect the widows and orphans, I have... set up these my precious words... as king of righteousness."[2]

Similar conditions apply to the people of Israel. In the Bible the condensed morality of the Ten Commandments presents, both systematically and didactically, a summary of the basic idea of how one should behave. On the one hand, the Commandments are a combination of minimal, historically-derived instructions for the individual's behavior, and on the other they posit themselves as fundamental components of Israel's divine relationship with Yahweh. In fact the Ten Commandments are seen as part of a contract between God and his people, whom he has chosen above all other peoples. As in the entire Middle East, in the land of the Bible too it is primarily a question of social consideration, although here it exists in other contexts. In Israel there is no land ownership. "The land is mine," says the Lord (Lev. 25:23). The territory that is divided up among the tribes is given to the people for cultivation only. In Israel land is not private property. The more wide-reaching significance of possessing goods and land can be seen, for example, in the legal regulation that even the poor ultimately have a right to use the land itself: the farmer may not strip his field down to the last pickings, nor take the gleanings from the vines. Thus the poor, and even wild animals, are to a certain extent co-owners of the land and must be able to take their share of the harvest. This comes into force, in particular, every seven years when according to the law of the Israelites the fields, vineyards, and olive groves may not be harvested by the owner at all.[3]

The Ten Commandments may have their literary home in the Bible, but their origins in the story of Mount Sinai are to be understood as a myth not as history. Here many details of the individual's everyday behavior are prescribed or forbidden. In the Ten Commandments not-doing occupies a more central position than its opposite. Once divorced from their diverse origins, these texts tend above all towards the regulation of social relationships between individuals, and towards property. The prohibitions against killing, adultery and stealing protect the neighbor's rights to his life and to his own world. An older version of the Ten Commandments concerning Israel's equitable social system makes this point compellingly:

"Thou shalt not covet thy neighbor's house, thou shalt not covet thy neighbor's wife, nor his manservant, nor his maidservant, nor his ox, nor his ass, nor anything that is thy neighbor's" (Exod. 20:17). Any incursion into another person's basic rights to freedom is thus to be refrained from in the strictest possible way. The same applies to his honor and his privacy, that is his own world. The Ten Commandments also dictate that one should not lie. It is a question of honesty and respect, of truth and deference, of showing that one honors the dignity of one's neighbor. These fundamental ethical laws are related to actual deeds and are treated as crimes. Their aim is not-doing.

Later on, however, this purely legal regulation of external action erects a personal defensive wall between the level of pure thought and the resulting action. The mere thought of abnormal ideas, petty desires, and egotistical lusts should be banished. Goodness is to be established within the individual in order to anticipate any translation into evil action. We can clearly see how the realization of Biblical society is not dependent on legal formulations alone, but follows a didactic path of education towards goodness.

TRANSFORMATIONS

The involvement of good character in implementing
and safeguarding social regulations goes even further
in Israel. It looks beyond the individual's behavior to a
more comprehensive social vision, binding it together
through religion, intensified on the one hand through
the tradition and form of Assyrian contractual ideas
and on the other once again by Israel's religion. Such
a form can be seen in the Israelites' notion of agreement, in the pact between God and his people. In
this so-called deed of covenant the pact is structured
as a contract between Yahweh and Israel. For both
sides, agreements and conditions are realized in freedoms and obligations. This is at once a curse and a
blessing. He who keeps to the contractually regulated
commandments and God's word in his devotions, and
refrains from breaching any of them, receives bless-
ings and happiness; by contrast he who offends
against them, is cursed.

Subsequently, these contractual regulations are ele-
vated to the level of religious festivals. They are offi-
cially celebrated and renewed each year. With regard
to the social institution of the Ten Commandments,
religious ritual and mythological tradition consoli-
date into a social "pact," and into the inner attitude of
the individual. This then leads to the "statutes" that

precede the Commandments. They are a reminder that God liberated the Israelites from Egypt, and they forbid heathen images and religions. In this way they specifically inculcate the Commandments into the entire people, as well as into each individual, and translate the entire contract into an attitude of religious devotion: "Then beware lest thou forget the Lord, which brought thee forth out of the land of Egypt, from the house of bondage. Thou shalt fear the Lord thy God, and serve him, and shalt swear by his name. Ye shall not go after other gods, of the gods of the people which are round about you" (Deut. 6:12–14).

Such ideas serve to personalize the Ten Commandments. Out of a legal framework a relationship of trust is created, a connection in the form of a partnership. The individual Commandments are sublimated into a common concern. Anything that could damage the covenant between God and the individuals among his people is prohibited. Even more importantly, anything that contradicts the covenant is to be avoided and to be eradicated from society. Social ostracism leads to fear; transgression leads to sacrilege, crime, turning away from God, and sin—indeed mortal sin.

What began as regulation and static equilibrium was always in danger of being understood as formal and reified. The Prophets and Jesus constantly stood up to this: an effort reflected in Jesus's teachings in the New Testament in the ideal of fulfilling the form and meaning of the Commandments. This fulfillment is brought to life through following Jesus's critical awakening into a new age, a following that is ultimately only possible through love, through being prepared to place oneself and one's own aims in the service of others. Only in this way can a free life be realized. This is why in the New Testament the return to God takes the form of looking after the meaning of the Commandments—a return to God in the heart and the whole person. In essence such a return consists in the ability to understand one's own dependencies and abnormal inclinations and to let go of them. In following Jesus, the Christian agrees to the requirement of spending an hour with Jesus, walking with him, and resisting the tension between reality that is hoped for and that which exists.[4] But in the history of Christianity Jesus's ground-breaking new departure and way forward really constantly lapses again and again into formal stagnation, despite all action and change.

As Humanism and the Reformation dawned, a new, sustainable kind of private piety developed, the so-called *Devotio Moderna*. It originated partly in mystical

initiatives from the Middle Ages, but was also sup-
ported later by the emerging Humanism of the 15th
century, with centers in the lands of the Habsburg
Empire, Spain, the Netherlands, the Lower Rhine
region and in Westphalia. At its heart lay the individual's personal attitude towards how they lead their life
and how they believe. This form of Christian Humanism launched many new initiatives within the
Church, and in particular a more radical version of
the Reformation.

Personal piety and inwardly following Jesus's
example, both in everyday life and spiritually, became
the principle of a new way of thinking and living.
These orientations provided an inner alternative to
overcoming the dominance of a unified existence
within the Orders. Reformist branches of the old
Orders, the foundation of new women's and men's
movements and of lay communities, were the fruits of
this period. Alongside many impressive figures, this
philosophy crystallized around two individuals in
particular: at the beginning, the theologian and
preacher Geert Groote (1340–84) from Deventer; and
later, in the monk Thomas à Kempis (1380–1471).

With what remained of his assets, Groote bought a
house and founded a lay community where women
from young girls to widows lived together in obe-

dience, poverty and chastity, without taking the regular vows associated with an Order. À Kempis was an extremely prolific writer. But his main work concerns the profoundly radical *De Imitatione Christi* [*The Imitation of Christ*]. This compelling and easily understandable text is one of the most popular books of all time, alongside the Bible. Ever since the 16th century countless editions have been published in almost all world languages; in German alone there must have been between 3,500 and 4,000 editions. The significance of following Christ resides not only in a mystical praxis that can be seen in everyday life but also in the fact that even non-Christians find very valuable suggestions on how to live in this book. Openness to people's everyday lives, clarity, and a concrete application and translation into one's own life characterize many publications of this time, including Ignatius of Loyola's *Spiritual Exercises*, a handbook for course leaders which was pioneering for many people who wanted to change from mental dependency to a life of honest responsibility.

The spirit of this personalization of religion, the invention of printing, and the entrepreneurial boom in influential international printers, such as the Plantin-Moretus publishing house in Antwerp, brought the "new thinking" to art, science, music, and literature as well. Albrecht Dürer's *Apocalypse*, printed in Nuremberg in two editions, is only one of many path-breaking beginnings. The easily disseminable printing of pamphlets espousing all opinions promoted free speech and critical argument, and culminated ultimately in spreading the energy of the new thinking. However, life and change continued, transforming and pervading the most diverse cultural areas while lapsing again and again into sclerotic ways of thought, prohibitions, paternalism, and paralysis—even despair.

THE IMPACT OF THE TEN COMMANDMENTS TODAY

Today the Ten Commandments are subject to the hectic pace of social development and modern life. A long time ago they were taken out of the hands of rulers and are now subject to the elected representatives of the people in democratic societies. The way conscience is created has also changed, and has become the subject of education. However it is the individual's democratic task to deal with the constant advance of ethically relevant social change. New realities strive to be acknowledged, as do personal responses to the burning questions of the time.

In this context religious locations, parishes, and communities play a decisive role in maintaining sacred spaces for silent concentration and personal reflection. Increasingly, they have developed into places for contemplation and meditation, where the outcome can be the opposite of a hasty action, namely the courage of not-doing, and the well thought-out refusal to do what is expected.

Both external and internal space belongs, like time, to the basic conditions of man. It can be accessible and open to the whole world, or completely closed in a massive block. In considering space we must distinguish between the container and the contained. From an architectonic point of view space is initially empty, albeit conceived in anticipation of its possible function. Design, construction, building materials, textures and, above all, light create a space and determine its character. But beyond this it must be configured and brought to life by the individual or group of people who want to inhabit it. Alongside an emotional dimension, space has a primarily conceptual dimension as a space of consciousness, imagination, or art. In such spaces feelings, knowledge and creative action are negotiated as a whole.

The specific task of a sacred space is to break down, move, and inform the mood of a visitor, while messages of faith conveyed through images can only disturb because they are unexpected. The individual who enters such a space wants to achieve stillness. His feelings should move outwards, liberated by the atmosphere of the space. In these places the individual first wants to find himself, then perhaps his God, and possibly ultimately a particular insight or message. But the awakening of his own experience is what drives the desire to feel his way or struggle beyond himself. He must move in this direction in the spirit of self-questioning.

Silence is the beginning of questioning. Emptiness is its foundation. All energy and movement stops oscillating. Time slows down and extends. The inner gaze focuses on the center of the body, on calm and tranquility, on serenity and equanimity. In this place everything lives from the silence—far removed from drama and stress. The haunting Thuringian painter Gerhard Altenbourg (1926–89), harassed and banned for many years in East Germany, was one of those artists who thrive on silence. Speaking on one occasion about drawing, he said this was where he stepped out of time, while simultaneously entering a continuum of those who had realized themselves before him.

In silence, man plunges into his foundations and seeks a foothold in the "eternal now." Here—amid the fullness of time—the empty, sacred space imparts contemplation and stability, and shows the way where being unfolds itself into a question. It is the question as a question. Like silence, the question belongs fundamentally to the human self. Only when the individual becomes questionable himself, when he looks into himself and redeems himself from himself, can he understand himself—in his location in space and time, in the question about himself and about his freedom. Man asks questions even without expressing them. He cannot avoid them, as his very life *is* the question.

In the wake of such self-transcendence the questioner reaches beyond himself and perhaps even beckons God to come to him. God is an experience in the form of a question; for what the word God means can initially only be described through a question. When man directs himself to the whole of the world and to life, God emerges in the question. Thus God lives in the question, but at the same time remains secret and hidden. He is questionable and present, but remains the *deus absconditus*, the hidden God.

No artist created an art of the question as determinedly as American James Lee Byars (1921–97). As

an artist, he takes up the position of a practically oriented, questioning art. For him, man realizes himself
in questions. As purposeful and answer-oriented
questioning may normally be, for Byars the focus of
his understanding of questioning lies essentially in
the act of questioning itself, not in questioning as the
search for answers. He boldly extends the question
from the realm of logic and language into that of art;
indeed he elevates the question conceptually into an
artistic form. The question is an aesthetic object that
exists for its own sake. In his art Byars questions the
question itself and awakens in the questioner the special quality of his consciousness, namely keeping
everything one has in mind open to the world and
thus being open to everything. Ultimately this artist
understands the question to be sufficient unto itself.
It does not live in terms of the answer, but from its
own impetus, from the impulse towards knowledge
and understanding. The question provides immediate
evidentness of a level of anticipation and intuition.
While the latter may be uncertain or fluctuating they
make the questioner receptive to external stimuli and
inspirations, open to the possibility of divine inspi-
ration. This is the prophetic consolation that can cut
through vagueness and check uncertainty.

From a Christian perspective the question of God is resolved in this world. In the in-spiration of the *Word*, God reveals himself out of divinity and distance into nearness and humanity. In the Bible it is St. Paul's Epistle to the Philippians that explains this idea, when, according to Paul, Jesus sets aside all divinity and becomes a man, a simple man. Silently he "dwells among men." In his silent reckoning with God Christ's life brings God to Earth, praying and questioning from the heights of pure concepts and garrulous theories into the soft "heart of flesh," where man himself is the holy space of faith in the silent rhythm of his heart.

This coexistence of both mysticism and questioning is the center of all energy for life—and yet remains uncertain in its certainties. In the continual exchange between question and answer, caught between knowledge and belief, always broken by doubt, man can perceive the transcendent in inner evidentness. Then he seeks to discern its vague contours: in the fullness of reflection, in expanding silence, and or also in wordless questioning. Ultimately he dares to grasp the "unknown" in the inner space of his faith. But is this where it finds a foothold, an atmospheric space?

Today many people who are searching conceive of sacred space not so much as a place of answers but more as an energy-filled space for seeking and questioning. This space should give the individual the strength to ask his personal questions and to find harmony between himself and the world, his body, and his space, doubting and questioning, skeptical and listening. In this way inner certainties can be perceived and constructed anew. Space that is created sensitively is simply trying to capture and concentrate atmospheres. And if it finds a creative form, it lets the manifestations shine out—nothing more than this, but this would be everything.

The Spanish sculptor Eduardo Chillida (1924–2002) conceives his art as a creation, even an embodiment of space. His aim is to visualize space, to make it experienceable. To do this he turns to philosophy. Permanently moving, he creates space anew again and again, charging it with intuition and feeling. Inside each space he locates the center within an empty middle. All his sculptural activity is focused on this. It acts like a spiritual center and activates much more than the viewer's optical powers. Years ago, when asked how he makes sense of this spiritual, living space, Chillida answered with these often quoted words: "Space? […] I could compare it with breath that makes the form swell up and then contract, that opens in the form the space of vision—inaccessible and hidden from the world outside. [...] This space must be able to be perceived as well as the form in which it is manifested. It has expressive qualities. It sets the material that encompasses it in motion, determines its proportions, scans and orders its rhythms. It must find in us its correspondences, its echoes; it must possess a kind of spiritual dimension."[5]

Within spaces understood in such a way new attitudes and their inner commandments can emerge freely, even the enactment of a specific commandment of not-doing.

Notes

1. Cited in Norbert Lohfink, "Die richtige Gesellschaft" in *Kirchenträume. Reden gegen den Trend* (Freiburg: Herder, 1982), p. 68. The Frankfurt-based Bible scholar Norbert Lohfink has referred repeatedly to these connections in the concrete text as well as from a historical point of view. The present author is grateful to Norbert Lohfink for relevant information in the above context.

2. Ibid.

3. Cf. Exod. 23:10f; Lev. 19:9f, 25:2–7; Deut. 24:19–22.

4. Mark 10:17–24.

5. Cited first by the Swiss art historian Peter Frey in an early catalogue by the Paris gallery Maeght-Lelong,

Chillida. Sculptures de terre (Zürich: Maeght Lelong, 1985), pp. 13 ff.

CHAPTER 13

"NOT-DOING" IN MARINA
ABRAMOVIĆ'S WORK *512 HOURS*

HANS-ULRICH OBRIST AND MARINA ABRAMOVIĆ

Hans-Ulrich Obrist: I am so excited, Marina, that
we can do this interview this morning. It's half-time;
it's actually beyond half-time now. It's the second day
over half-time of your *512 Hours*[1] at the Serpentine.
How do you feel?

Marina Abramović: So many things are really happening and things are changing and the most important thing in this process is that I'm changing, because
in the beginning I didn't know how this perfor-

mance—I didn't even know what to call it—would actually develop because I didn't have rules, I didn't have any kind of starting point except that the public should come to the space and something was going to happen. That can go in every different direction. It can be a complete failure or it can go ways that I didn't expect.

But now, as we are halfway through, I can say that a miracle is happening. Somehow the public come in, without any instructions and they are coming with these headphones to completely block the sound, and in less than ten minutes they settle down. There is some kind of mutual understanding in the group of what has to be done. They know they are coming here for their own experience; they are not coming to look at something. They are coming here to be part of something.

So in the beginning I spent lots of energy trying to balance these energies in the three different spaces and making sure that everybody is doing what they're supposed to do. But now more and more I'm blending in; more and more I'm taking this position of the public itself. So I am just part of them and sometimes you can't find me because I will be counting rice or walking slowly or I will be just sitting on the chair with closed eyes for a long period of time or standing in the center.

That blending in is completely new ground for performance art, when an artist is not anymore present in the way he was before.

HUO: What is fascinating is how the work changes over time, because when it started—actually I remember the first hour where basically you put visitors into the room—there were no props used at the beginning. However, from the very beginning you wanted it to be silent. That has been persistent, consistent, the idea of actual silence. Can you tell us a little bit about that main rule of the game, of silence? Why silence? And then also within the silence how, little by little, you change the props? I think what you're doing here in London has a lot to do with the question of inaction as a form of action because it is not about a form of actionism; it is inaction as action. Can you talk a little bit about this idea?

MA: I see the silence as an extremely important condition of everything because I think that it is some extension of any decision that you have to take. When you come into the museum you have to put your watch and computer and your phones in the lockers. Then the next thing is that you are actually cut off from communication, cut off from time and the next thing is you are actually cut off from noise. So when you enter the silence in the space and you put this extra silence in your ears you automatically are in a different space, in a different zone. You are in a kind of parallel reality and that really helps people to focus.

Then I realized that if you don't have any props and I just place you against the wall it's too soon and people won't stay long enough because our mind doesn't work that way. We need preparation; we need a certain amount of time to spend with props that are just the tools in order to get to that kind of concentration.

A simple example is the long walk. I suggest to walk around the room seven times. Seven times is very important because it's based on repetition and it's a very ancient exercise. Then the body gets the same amount of oxygen each time because it's slow and this is the way the mind gets stabilized. I always compare our mind to a Ferrari. We are running with the mind but the body can be slow. But the idea is how actually to create the situation when the mind and the body are at the same speed.

This can only happen through repetition. The first time you walk around the room you are conscious of the body, the second time you are conscious of your walk, you are kind of dis-balanced, the third time because of the silence you listen to your heart beating, and then fourthly your mind starts to slow down. But it's only during the fifth, sixth, or seventh time that you actually get to that point when time doesn't matter anymore, that actually the act of walking is everything. Then you're going back to this presence. Then you get into this incredible moment of observation just looking in front of you at the floor, and to me it becomes almost like Agnes Martin's paintings when she just observed the floor of her room and how the light and the dust reaches the ray of light on the surface.

So you become particular about the details. Then you get particular about your movement and then this kind of fluidity starts happening so it's like you're floating in space. Then slowly you're reaching this white wall and then you can stand in front of the white wall as long as you want because you're prepared to do that. Then you turn again, and again you're going through the same emotion and again it's this white wall.

Then that whole process really brings you to actually—to the beginning of that game which I propose. Come to the Serpentine and face the white wall. But we need the tools to get ready.

HUO: At the beginning you did not have a plan for

this *512 Hours*, but that it started with nothing, it started with inaction. Can you talk a little bit about that?

MA: The older you get, the more closed you get, so the curiosity of the child is lost, and here I'm asking you to go back to this moment of being a child again, to be—to allow yourself to be touched, to allow yourself to hold the hand of this total stranger and bring you to that experience with complete openness. It's really hard to create this transition because people are not used to it, because here we're not talking about a temple, this is not a temple, this is just a museum, it's a space to be shown art. When art is removed and there's no art to be shown you become actually the work itself and the object and the subject.

HUO: The idea also of de-linking in our age is so important—that we have moments of de-linking. And here in your *512 Hours* is a very radical moment of de-linking. You basically take all these devices away from people—the iPhone, the camera, the cell phone, the Blackberry. What prompted this idea?

MA: Well it's incredibly important, this idea of getting time for yourself and all our experience now is experienced through the media. Because people, if they have the camera they will go and they will make photographs with the phone, they will go home and look at these photographs in order to have a direct experience; the experience will be replaced by the media.

So here we take media away and then you really only focus on yourself. If we ask you to close your eyes, you don't see. If you put on the headphones, you don't hear. So really you are deprived of two senses. You actually have to experience it with your body. I want you to see with your body like a blind person; he can see with the body.

To me it was really important that this works. I interviewed this small, little kid who is eleven years old and is called Oscar, and he came here with his father and mother very regularly. I asked the mother and father whether he wanted to come. They said yes, he asks us every day if he can come here. They can't bring him here every day but at least every three or four days he is present.

He would go to the middle of the space and just stand there with closed eyes for a long period of time, or do the long walks more than seven times. So when we asked him what this brings to his own life he told us when he comes from school—because school is so demanding and he's very nervous—he starts to run around the room and then he's settling down. After this experience now he will go to a small room and he will go and stand just in the middle with eyes closed for a long period of time, and after this he will do anything else.

For me that makes all the difference. If this kid of eleven gets it then I know I'm doing a good job.

HUO: There is also a form of connection, which is interesting. So on the one hand there is disconnection because people—visitors—disconnect from their devices, but they find another form of connection. It's interesting because the exhibition as a ritual is very much a liberal ritual. People can come and go when they want. As Dorothea von Hantelmann writes in the new book on exhibitions: it's not like in theater, in that one has a situation where one person communicates to a crowd; it's a more individualized ritual and you stick to that individualized ritual because it's a one-to-one situation. However, you create a new form of connection, and that form of connection means people don't just stand for ten or fifteen seconds in front of the actor, they actually spend a lot of time. We have got people who come here every day. Maybe it's interesting to talk a little bit about that new form of connection.

MA: You know, that's really important because in a

performance, especially in the 1970s, there was lots of bad work. So you are actually in a situation where you're sitting for a long period of time looking at something that you are bored with or you don't want to look at, but because of the sitting situation you are kind of forced to. I think that already, even when working with Ulay in the 1980s with a work such as *Nightsea Crossing*, we removed the situation of the sitting; we just thought it wasn't necessary anymore. Then later on I followed this attitude always, that actually it is the public who decide what amount of time they should spend looking at the work. That freedom is essential so that you can spend one minute or you can spend three hours; it's all up to you. It depends how much energy you have in order to do it.

So that's really important, to remove that kind of stage situation and to have this kind of freedom. Here it's even a step further because here there is—in each of these exercises—there is the freedom that you can stop any time you want. But the thing that happened here, there is some kind of quality of energy which is addictive so that people stay longer than they actually planned because the energy of the other person supports his own energy and it makes this kind of global energy together. It's like—I can compare it to when you never exercise in your own home but you go to the gym because of the atmosphere—it's about exercise so you'll do much more in the gym than at home.

So here, in a way, it's similar. You come here and you sit on the chair with closed eyes or stand on the platform and you never do this in your own home, except Oscar, the little kid.

By the way, it's wonderful what one girl came and told me two days ago. She said, "You gave us so little when I came into the gallery, but I came out with so much."

HUO: That's a great conclusion. Thank you so much.

London, July 21, 2014

Notes

1. *512 Hours.* A new durational performance by Marina Abramović, June 11 to August 25, 2014, Serpentine Gallery, London.

CONTRIBUTORS

Marina Abramović was born in 1946 in Belgrade, Serbia. She moved to Amsterdam in 1976 and has lived in New York since 2001. Her pioneering works of performance art have made her the subject of numerous solo and group exhibitions worldwide at institutions including Kunstmuseum and Grosse Halle, Bern, Switzerland and La Gallera, Valencia, Spain (1998); Solomon R. Guggenheim Museum, New York (2005); Museum of Modern Art, New York (2010); the Garage Centre for Contemporary Culture, Moscow (2011); Kunsthalle, Vienna (2012). Abramović's work was also included in documenta VI, VII, and IX (1977, 1982, and 1992); also Venice Biennale 1976 and 1997, with the exhibition *Balkan Baroque* in the latter earning her the Golden Lion Award for Best Artist.

Prof.em. Dr.sc.tc.hc.phil.hc. Bazon Brock is Emeritus Professor of Aesthetics and Cultural Education at the Bergische Universität in Wuppertal, Germany, and was previously Professor at Hamburg University of Fine Arts (1965–76) and the University of Applied Arts, Vienna (1977–80). In 1992 he was awarded an honorary doctorate at ETH (Swiss Federal Institute for Technology, Zürich) and in 2012 at the Hochschule für Gestaltung, Karlsruhe. Between 1968 and 1992 he led the documenta schools for visitors. He currently runs courses for "professional citizens" at the Karlsruhe University of Arts and Design (Rector: Peter Sloterdijk). He is a member of the Institut für theoretische Kunst, Universalpoesie und Prognostik and founder of the Amt für Arbeit an unlösbaren Problemen und Maßnahmen der hohen Hand, Berlin.

Dr. Corinne Michaela Flick studied both law and literature, taking American studies as her subsidiary. She gained her Dr. phil. in 1989. She has worked as in-house lawyer for Bertelsmann Buch AG and Amazon.com. In 1998 she became General Partner in Vivil GmbH und Co. KG, Offenburg. She is Founder and Chair of the Convoco Foundation.

Dr. Flick is Chair of the Board of Trustees of the Aspen Institute, Germany; member of the board of the Alfred Herrhausen Society, the International Forum of Deutsche Bank; member of the board of the Osterfestspiele, Salzburg; and a member of the Executive Committee of the International Council of the Tate Gallery, London.

Prof. Dr. Gert-Rudolf Flick holds a Ph.D. in law from the Ludwig-Maximilian University, Munich and is a scholar of European art history covering the period from the 16th to 19th centuries. He is a Visiting Professor in the Department of Art History at the University of Buckingham. The former publisher of *Apollo* art magazine is a recognized collector of Old Masters, Italian *vedutà*, and 17th–19th-century silver. Professor Flick is the author of *Missing Masterpieces—Lost Works of Art, 1450–1900* (2002) and *Masters and Pupils: The Artistic Succession from Perugino to Manet 1480–1880* (2008).

Prof. Dr. Peter M. Huber gained his Ph.D. Dr. jur. in 1987 and his postdoctoral qualification in constitutional and administrative law in 1991. He was Professor of Public Law in Augsburg. In 1992–2001 he was Professor of Constitutional and Administrative Law, European Law, Public, Commercial and Environmental Law in Jena. He was Chair of Public Law and European Integration Law in Bayreuth from 2001 to 2002.

Since 2002 he has held the Chair of Public Law and Political Philosophy in Munich.

From 2009 to 2010 Professor Huber was Interior Minister for Thuringia, and in 2010 he was made a Judge in Germany's Federal Constitutional Court.

Among his publications are: *Grundrechtsschutz durch Organisation und Verfahren als Kompetenzproblem in der Gewaltenteilung und im Bundesstaat* (1987); *Konkurrenzschutz im Verwaltungsrecht* (1991); *Recht der Europäischen Integration* (second edition, 2002); *Klarere Verantwortungsteilung von Bund, Ländern und Kommunen?* (2004); *Staat und Wissenschaft* (2008); *Beiträge zu Juristenausbildung und Hochschulrecht* (2010). He is Joint Editor of the *Handbuch Ius Publicum Europaeum*, vols. I–IV (2007–11).

Prof. Dr. Kai A. Konrad gained his doctorate (1990) and his postdoctoral qualification (1993) at the University of Munich. He has taught and undertaken research at the Universities of Munich, Bonn, Bergen (Norway), and the University of California, Irvine. From 1994 to 2009 he was Professor of Economics at the Free University Berlin, and from 2001 to 2009 he was Director of the Social Science Research Center, Berlin. Since January 2011 he has been Director at the Max Planck Institute for Tax Law and Public Finance. He is co-editor of the *Journal of Public Economics*, and serves on the editorial board of a number of other international academic journals. He is author of more than 80 articles in international economic and political journals. He is Chairman of the Council of Scientific Advisors to the German Ministry of Finance.

Prof. Dr. Stefan Korioth gained his doctorate in law in 1990 and completed his postdoctoral qualification in public and constitutional law. From 1996 to 2000 he was Professor of Public Law, Constitutional History, and Theory of Government at Greifswald. In 2000 he accepted the Chair of Public and Ecclesiastical Law at LMU, Munich. His publications include *Integration und Bundesstaat* (1990), *Der Finanzausgleich zwischen Bund und Ländern* (1997), *Grundzüge des Staatskirchenrechts* (with B. Jean d'Heur, 2000), and *Das Bundesverfassungsgericht* (with Klaus Schlaich, 9th edition, 2012).

Prof. Dr. Friedhelm Mennekes S.J. is a Jesuit who studied philosophy, political science, and theology in Bonn, Munich, and Frankfurt am Main. In 1971 he studied for his doctorate under K.D. Bracher in Bonn. In 1979 he gained his postdoctoral qualification in practical theology and the sociology of religion in Frankfurt am Main. He was then appointed Professor in Frankfurt and Pastor in Cologne. Since 1979 he has been curating modern art exhibitions in churches. In 1985 he founded a center for contemporary art and music, the Kunst-Station Sankt Peter Köln. Here Friedhelm Mennekes engages directly with artists such as Beuys, Bacon, Boltanski, Chillida, Dumas, Hrdlicka, Kruger, Rainer, Sherman, and Trockel, among others. Today his work still aims to create radical encounters between modern art, music, and religion. For Mennekes, the idea of Christian art as such does not exist (see www.artandreligion.de).

Hans Ulrich Obrist is Co-director of the Serpentine Galleries, London. Prior to this, he was curator of the Musée d'Art Moderne de la Ville, Paris. Since his first show *World Soup (The Kitchen Show)* in 1991 he has curated more than 250 exhibitions.

In 2009 Obrist was made Honorary Fellow of the Royal Institute of British Architects (RIBA), and in 2011 received the CCS Bard Award for Curatorial Excellence. Obrist has lectured internationally at academic and art institutions, and is contributing editor to several magazines and journals.

Obrist's recent publications include *A Brief History of Curating, Everything You Always Wanted to Know About Curating But Were Afraid to Ask, Do It: The Compendium, Think Like Clouds, Ai Weiwei Speaks, Ways of Curating,* and new volumes of his *Conversation Series.*

Prof. Dr. Christoph G. Paulus studied law at Munich, taking his doctorate in law in 1980. His post-doctoral qualification, gained in 1991, was in civil law, civil procedure, and Roman law, for which he was awarded the Medal of the University of Paris II. He received his LL.M. at Berkley in 1983/1984 and returned to Berkeley between 1989 and 1990 as a recipient of a Feodor Lynen Stipend from the Humboldt Foundation. In 1992–94 he was Associate Professor at Augsburg, and from the summer semester 1994 he was at the Law Faculty of the Humboldt University in Berlin, becoming Dean of the Faculty in 2008–10. In 2009 he was made Director of the Research Center Institute for Interdisciplinary Restructuring, and Consultant to the International Monetary Fund and the World Bank. Among other roles he is Member (and Director) of the International Insolvency Institute of the American College of Bankruptcy and the International Association for Procedural Law. Since 2006 he has been advisor on insolvency law to the German delegation to UNCITRAL. He is on the editorial board of the *Zeitschrift für Wirtschaftsrecht* (ZIP), the *Norton Annual Review of International Insolvency*, and the *International Insolvency Law Review*, among other journals.

Prof. Jörg Rocholl, Ph.D. is President of ESMT European School of Management and Technology in Berlin and holds the Ernst & Young Chair in Governance and Compliance. Professor Rocholl graduated from the Universität Witten/Herdecke, where he earned a degree in economics (with honors). After completing his Ph.D. at Columbia University in New York, he was named an Assistant Professor at the University of North Carolina at Chapel Hill. Professor Rocholl has researched and taught at ESMT since 2007 and was appointed President of ESMT in 2011. He is a member of the Economic Advisory Board of the German Federal Ministry of Finance, Research Professor at the ifo Institute in Munich, and Duisenberg Fellow of the European Central Bank (ECB).

Prof. Dr. Dr. h.c. Wolfgang Schön studied law and economics studies at the University of Bonn, and was awarded his doctorate at Bonn in 1985. In 1992 he received his postdoctoral qualification in civil law, commercial, corporate, and tax law in Bonn. He was Professor at the University of Bielefeld from 1992 to 1996, and Director of the Institute for Tax Law and of the Centre of European Commercial Law, Bonn from 1996 to 2002. Since 2002 he has been Director and Scientific Member of the Max Planck Institute for Intellectual Property, Competition, and Tax Law in Munich. He has been Honorary Professor of Civil, Commercial, Corporate, and Tax Law at the Ludwig-Maximilian University, Munich since 2002. From 2008 to 2014 Professor Schön was Vice-President of the Max Planck Society. Since 2014 he has been Vice-President of the German Research Foundation (DFG).

Prof. Roger Scruton, Ph.D. is currently a Senior Research Fellow of Blackfriars Hall, Oxford and Senior Fellow at the Ethics and Public Policy Center, Washington DC. He was for a while employed by Birkbeck College in the University of London, but since 1990 has been self-employed. He is author of over 40 books, including works of criticism, political theory, and aesthetics, as well as novels and short stories. His writings include *The Aesthetics of Music* (1997), *Death-Devoted Heart: Sex and the Sacred in Wagner's* Tristan and Isolde (2003), *Understanding Music* (2009), *The Face of God* (2011), *The Soul of the World* (2014), and *Notes from Underground* (2014). Roger Scruton is a Fellow of the Royal Society of Literature, a Fellow of the European Academy of Arts and Sciences, and a Fellow of the British Academy.

Prof. Dr. Pirmin Stekeler-Weithofer studied German, theoretical linguistics, philosophy (MA 1975), and mathematics (diploma 1977) in Konstanz, Berlin, Prague, and Berkeley. He received his doctorate in 1984, and his postdoctoral qualification in 1987. Since 1992 he has been Professor of Theoretical Philosophy at the University of Leipzig. He has taught and researched widely abroad in Campinas, São Paulo, Brazil (1988), Pittsburgh, PA (1990–92, 2006), Swansea, Great Britain (1997/98), and held the Theodor Heuss Chair in New York (2002). Since 1994 he has been Director of the Humanities Center, and since 2009 Director of the Center for Higher Studies at the University of Leipzig. Since 1998 he has been a member and since 2008 President of the Saxonian Academy of Sciences in Leipzig. He is Vice-President of the International Hegel Association and the International Ludwig Wittgenstein Society. Since 2005 he has been a member of the Selection Committee for Research Grants at the Alexander von Humboldt Foundation.

Corinne Michaela Flick (Ed.)

Dealing with Downturns: Strategies in Uncertain Times

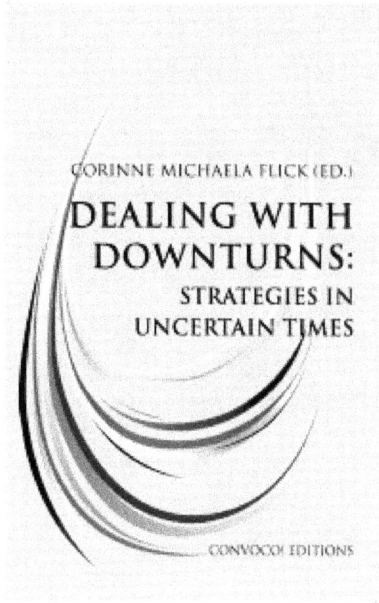

2014

ISBN: 978-0-957-295-889

With contributions by: Jens Beckert, Bazon Brock, Saul David, Gerd Gigerenzer, Paul Kirchhof, Kai A. Konrad, Stefan Korioth, Christoph G. Paulus, Jörg Rocholl and Burkhard Schwenker

Corinne Michaela Flick (Ed.)

Collective Law-Breaking–A Threat to Liberty

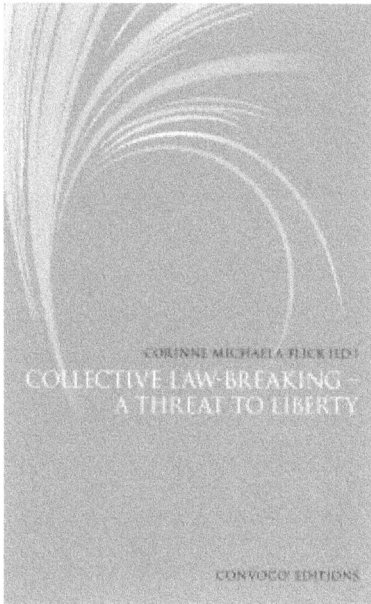

2013

ISBN: 978-0-9572958-5-8

With contributions by: Shaukat Aziz,
Roland Berger, Christoph G. Paulus, Ingolf
Pernice, Wolfgang Schön, Hannes Siegrist /
Pirmin Stekeler-Weithofer and Jürgen Stark

www.ingramcontent.com/pod-product-compliance
Lightning Source LLC
Chambersburg PA
CBHW060040030426
42334CB00019B/2408